Ready to Test

SKILLS & STRATEGIES

AMERICAN
EDUCATION
PUBLISHING™

An imprint of Carson-Dellosa Publishing
Greensboro, NC

American Education Publishing™
An imprint of Carson-Dellosa Publishing LLC
P.O. Box 35665
Greensboro, NC 27425 USA

ISBN 978-1-60996-535-8

01-363117784

Table of Contents

Language Arts
Reading

Chapter 1: Vocabulary

Chapter 2: Reading Comprehension

Language Arts
Language

Chapter 3: Mechanics

Chapter 4: Grammar

Chapter 5: Usage

Chapter 6: Writing

Math

Chapter 7: Concepts

Chapter 8: Computation

Chapter 9: Geometry

Chapter 10: Measurement

Chapter 11: Applications

Letter to Parents

Dear Parents and Guardians:

The *Ready to Test* series will prepare your child for standardized tests by providing him or her with test-taking tips and strategies for success. The sample questions and tests in this book will allow your child to gain familiarity with standardized tests, making him or her more comfortable on test day and, therefore, more likely to do well.

You can help your child with this important part of learning. Allow your child to become familiar with the testing strategies presented in this book. If your child gets stuck at any point when completing the book, encourage him or her to think of those tips to help determine what to do.

Time your child to help him or her learn time management when taking tests. On average, a lesson page in this book should take about 10 minutes to complete. A Practice Test should take about 45–60 minutes to complete. Keep in mind, however, that the goal is not how fast your child can complete each page. Instead, the goal is to provide practice and strategies for success on test day.

Below are some additional suggestions that will help your child make the most of *Ready to Test*:

- Provide a quiet place to work.
- Go over the work with your child.
- Tell your child he or she is doing a good job.
- Remind him or her to use the tips that are included throughout the book.

By preparing your child with test-taking tips and strategies, *Ready to Test* can help take the fear out of standardized tests and help your child achieve the best scores possible.

Introduction

About the Common Core State Standards

The Common Core State Standards Initiative is a state-led effort developed in collaboration with teachers, school administrators, and experts to provide a clear and consistent framework to prepare children for college and the workforce. The standards are based on the most effective models from states across the country. They provide teachers and parents with a common understanding of what students are expected to learn. Consistent standards will provide appropriate benchmarks for all students, regardless of where they live.

The Common Core State Standards provide a consistent, clear understanding of what students are expected to learn, so teachers and parents know how to help them. The standards are designed to be relevant to the real world, reflecting the knowledge and skills that children need for success in college and their future careers. With students fully prepared for the future, our communities and our country will be best positioned to compete successfully in the global economy.

These standards define the knowledge and skills students should have within their education so that they will graduate high school able to succeed in college and in workforce training programs. The standards:

- are aligned with college and work expectations.
- are clear, understandable, and consistent.
- include rigorous content and application of knowledge through high-order skills.
- build upon strengths and lessons of current state standards.
- are informed by other top-performing countries, so that all students are prepared to succeed in our global economy and society.
- are evidence-based.

Common Core Standards: Language Arts

The Language Arts standards focus on five key areas. Students who are proficient in these areas are able to demonstrate independence, build strong content knowledge, comprehend as well as critique, respond to the varying demands of the task, value evidence, use technology strategically and effectively, and understand other perspectives and cultures.

Reading

The Common Core Standards establish increasing complexity in what students must be able to read, so that all students are ready for the demands of college- and career-level reading. The standards also require the progressive development of reading comprehension, so that students are able to gain more from what they read.

Writing

The ability to write logical arguments based on substantive claims, sound reasoning, and relevant evidence is a cornerstone of the writing standards. Research is emphasized throughout the standards but most prominently in the writing strand, since a written analysis and presentation of findings is often critical.

Speaking and Listening

The standards require that students gain, evaluate, and present increasingly complex information, ideas, and evidence through listening and speaking, as well as through media.

Language

The standards expect that students will grow their vocabularies through a mix of conversations, direct instruction, and reading. The standards will help students determine word meanings, appreciate the nuances of words, and steadily expand their vocabulary of words and phrases.

Media and Technology

Skills related to media use are integrated throughout the standards, just as media and technology are integrated in school curriculum for life in the 21st century.

Common Core Standards: Math

The mathematically proficient student must be able to:

Make sense of problems and persevere in solving them. Mathematically proficient students start by thinking about the meaning of a problem and deciding upon the best way to find the solution. They think the problem through while solving it, and they continually ask themselves, "Does this make sense?"

Reason abstractly and quantitatively. Mathematically proficient students make sense of quantities and their relationships in problem situations. Quantitative reasoning entails an understanding of the problem at hand; paying attention to the units involved; considering the meaning of quantities, not just how to compute them; and knowing and using different properties of operations and objects.

Construct viable arguments and critique the reasoning of others. Mathematically proficient students understand and use stated assumptions, definitions, and previously established results in constructing arguments. Students at all grades can listen or read the arguments of others, decide whether they make sense, and ask useful questions to clarify or improve the arguments.

Model with mathematics. Mathematically proficient students can apply the math they've learned to solve problems arising in everyday life.

Use appropriate tools strategically. Mathematically proficient students consider the available tools when solving a mathematical problem and make appropriate decisions about when each of these tools might be helpful.

Attend to precision. Mathematically proficient students try to communicate precisely to others and in their own reasoning. They state the meaning of the symbols they choose. They calculate accurately and express answers efficiently.

Look for and make use of structure. Mathematically proficient students look closely to discern a pattern or structure. Students can also step back for an overview and shift perspective.

Look for and express regularity in repeated reasoning. Mathematically proficient students look for patterns and shortcuts. As they work to solve a problem, students continue to keep the big picture in mind while attending to the details. They continually evaluate whether or not their results make logical sense.

To learn more about the Common Core State Standards, visit corestandards.org.

Synonyms

Directions: Read each item. Choose the answer that means the same, or about the same, as the underlined word.

Example

a <u>delicious</u> pie

- (A) salty
- (B) bad
- (C) gentle
- (D) tasty

Answer: D

---

1. an <u>automobile</u> show

- (A) train
- (B) car
- (C) plane
- (D) wagon

2. a <u>faint</u> cry

- (F) soft
- (G) loud
- (H) sad
- (J) angry

3. an <u>ordinary</u> day

- (A) strange
- (B) memorable
- (C) rainy
- (D) usual

4. The castle flew a bright <u>banner</u>.

- (F) cloud
- (G) flag
- (H) balloon
- (J) talk

5. She found the store <u>entrance</u>.

- (A) cart
- (B) cashier
- (C) doorway
- (D) stairs

6. Zip was a strange <u>creature</u>.

- (F) floor
- (G) animal
- (H) cloth
- (J) doctor

Not sure about the right answer?

Try each answer choice in place of the underlined word. Choose the one that makes the most sense.

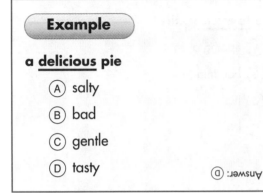

Synonyms

Directions: Read each item. Choose the answer that means the same, or about the same, as the underlined word.

1. a secret <u>bond</u>

(A) tie

(B) search

(C) trap

(D) light

2. <u>attend</u> a class

(F) skip

(G) pass

(H) like

(J) go to

3. a <u>towering</u> cliff

(A) tipping over

(B) handmade

(C) high

(D) low

Directions: Choose the best answer to complete each sentence.

4. A basement is like a _____.

(F) staircase

(G) attic

(H) kitchen

(J) cellar

5. To faint is to _____.

(A) bow

(B) pass out

(C) wake up

(D) pretend

6. To be disturbed is to be _____.

(F) upset

(G) calm

(H) joyful

(J) noisy

Your first answer choice is probably correct.

Don't change it unless you are sure another answer is better.

Antonyms

Directions: Read each item. Choose the answer that means the opposite of the underlined word.

Example

The ladder is <u>unsafe</u>.

- Ⓐ dangerous
- Ⓑ safe
- Ⓒ rickety
- Ⓓ scary

Answer: Ⓑ

1. **Joseph was <u>annoyed</u> with his cat.**
   - Ⓐ angry
   - Ⓑ worried
   - Ⓒ tired
   - Ⓓ satisfied

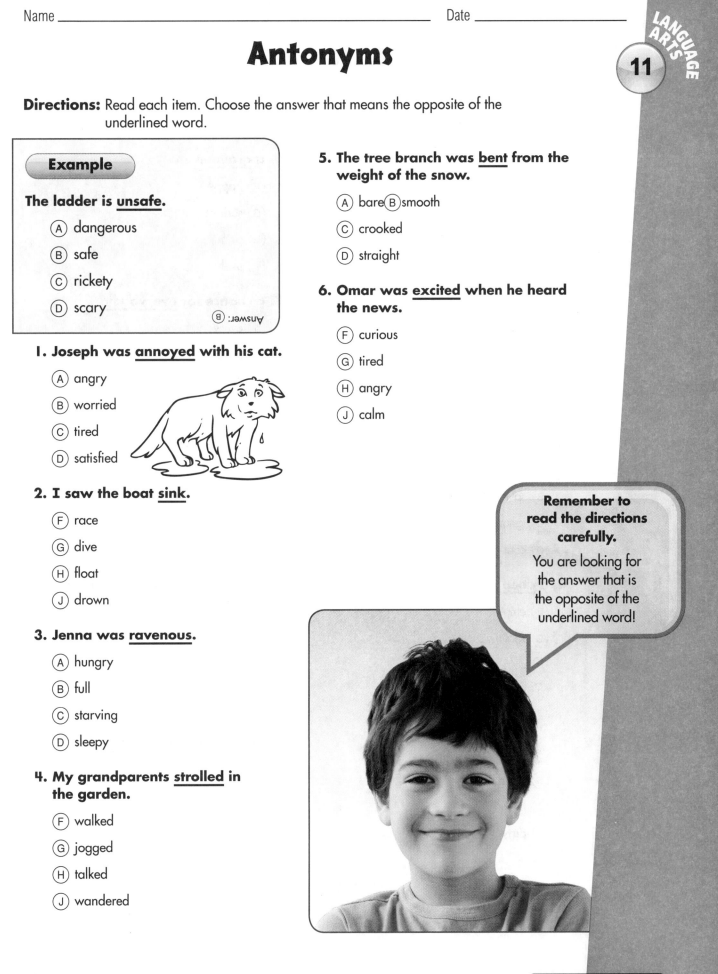

2. **I saw the boat <u>sink</u>.**
   - Ⓕ race
   - Ⓖ dive
   - Ⓗ float
   - Ⓙ drown

3. **Jenna was <u>ravenous</u>.**
   - Ⓐ hungry
   - Ⓑ full
   - Ⓒ starving
   - Ⓓ sleepy

4. **My grandparents <u>strolled</u> in the garden.**
   - Ⓕ walked
   - Ⓖ jogged
   - Ⓗ talked
   - Ⓙ wandered

5. **The tree branch was <u>bent</u> from the weight of the snow.**
   - Ⓐ bare
   - Ⓑ smooth
   - Ⓒ crooked
   - Ⓓ straight

6. **Omar was <u>excited</u> when he heard the news.**
   - Ⓕ curious
   - Ⓖ tired
   - Ⓗ angry
   - Ⓙ calm

Remember to read the directions carefully.

You are looking for the answer that is the opposite of the underlined word!

Antonyms

Directions: Read each item. Choose the answer that means the opposite of the underlined word.

1. **<u>destroy</u> a building**
   - (A) create
   - (B) imagine
   - (C) move
   - (D) hide

2. **a <u>narrow</u> doorway**
   - (F) broken
   - (G) small
   - (H) wide
   - (J) sturdy

3. **<u>spend</u> your money**
   - (A) lose
   - (B) save
   - (C) ignore
   - (D) consider

4. **a <u>deep</u> pool**
   - (F) empty
   - (G) shallow
   - (H) cold
   - (J) unusual

5. **a <u>polluted</u> stream**
   - (A) poisonous
   - (B) clean
   - (C) flowing
   - (D) dirty

6. **a <u>grave</u> event**
   - (F) happy
   - (G) serious
   - (H) grim
   - (J) likely

7. **a chance for <u>everybody</u>**
   - (A) everyone
   - (B) the crowd
   - (C) the class
   - (D) nobody

8. **a <u>hard</u> question**
   - (F) strange
   - (G) easy
   - (H) difficult
   - (J) rough

9. **My parents thought you were very <u>polite</u>.**
   - (A) rude
   - (B) tired
   - (C) odd
   - (D) fearful

10. **Was the watch <u>expensive</u>?**
    - (F) new
    - (G) cheap
    - (H) free
    - (J) comfortable

Multiple-Meaning Words

Directions: Read each pair of sentences. Choose the word that fits in the blank in both sentences.

Example

Mom told Zack not to _____ his sister.
The _____ at the party was delicious.

(A) shovel

(B) dig

(C) punch

(D) rake

Answer: C

1. The trees had rough _____.
The dog will _____ all day long.

(A) branches

(B) yap

(C) bark

(D) jump

2. Did the baby _____ the toy?
Mr. Ito wanted to take a _____.

(F) sleep

(G) lose

(H) ruin

(J) break

3. Dad gets a _____ every week.
I want to _____ my math homework.

(A) note

(B) redo

(C) check

(D) payment

4. There is a _____ on the front of my shirt.
Did you _____ the robin in the tree?

(F) mark

(G) spot

(H) notice

(J) stain

5. Mom works at a law _____ downtown.
I like to sleep with a _____ pillow, not a soft one.

(A) office

(B) rough

(C) building

(D) firm

6. Did you _____ the car here?
My sisters love to play at the _____.

(F) park

(G) pool

(H) leave

(J) playground

Name _____   Date _____

Multiple-Meaning Words

Directions: Find the answer in which the underlined word is used in the same way as it is in the box.

Example

This [kind] of plant is rare.

(A) Mrs. Rodriguez is kind.

(B) The kind man smiled.

(C) I like this kind of cereal.

(D) No one thinks that person is kind.

Answer: C

1. Lita rode every single ride at the county [fair].

(A) Granny's apple pie won first prize at the fair.

(B) Dad is always fair to my brother and me.

(C) It doesn't seem fair that it rains every weekend!

(D) Do you think the other team played a fair game?

2. Mr. Romanov is a very [patient] piano teacher.

(F) The dentist's last patient arrived at 5:00.

(G) Dr. Halliday's next patient is Maria Gomez.

(H) The patient sat in the waiting room for 10 minutes.

(J) It's hard to be patient when we've been waiting for an hour!

3. Finn's birthday cake was shaped like a [train].

(A) How long did it take you to train your puppy?

(B) The last train will be leaving at 11:30 tonight.

(C) Max will have to train the new employees.

(D) Kerry can train the dolphins to obey many commands.

4. The knight will [bow] to the queen.

(F) She tied a big bow on the gift.

(G) I know that I should bow to my dance partner.

(H) Did you see how the bow matched her dress?

(J) A bow is made of ribbon.

5. Put your [hand] on the table.

(A) Give Mr. Johnson a hand.

(B) The band deserves a hand for their music.

(C) Please give your little sister your hand.

(D) I have to hand it to you.

Words in Context

Directions: Read each item. Choose the answer that best fits in the blank.

Example

My mother used the garden _____ to wash the dog.

- (A) rake
- (B) seeds
- (C) hose
- (D) glove

Answer: (C)

1. The _____ roller coaster made us scream!

- (A) interesting
- (B) boring
- (C) slow
- (D) thrilling

2. The stormy weather will _____ all night.

- (F) change
- (G) continue
- (H) stop
- (J) knock

3. You should _____ this idea.

- (A) think
- (B) drive
- (C) consider
- (D) write

4. The _____ vase already has a chip in it.

- (F) latest
- (G) metal
- (H) fragile
- (J) useful

5. Before bed, Cleo writes about the day in her _____.

- (A) diary
- (B) desk
- (C) backpack
- (D) mind

6. Let me know when you _____ the entire book.

- (F) enjoy
- (G) replace
- (H) lose
- (J) complete

If two answer choices are the opposite of one another, one of them is probably correct.

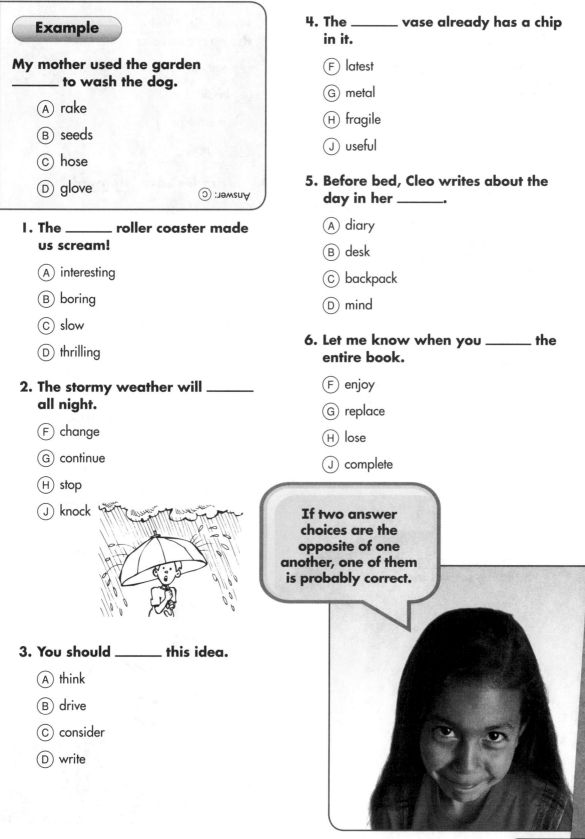

LANGUAGE ARTS

16

Words in Context

Directions: Find the word that means the same thing as the underlined word.

Example

Are you starting on your <u>journey</u>?

- (A) class
- (B) lesson
- (C) trip
- (D) vacation

Answer: (C)

1. Bring your paper and pencils so you can <u>sketch</u> the birds.

- (A) call
- (B) capture
- (C) draw
- (D) change

2. Can you <u>locate</u> the street on the map?

- (F) remove
- (G) forget
- (H) explain
- (J) find

3. I love to <u>observe</u> when my dad is building something.

- (A) measure
- (B) watch
- (C) return
- (D) decide

4. Please find <u>Volume</u> K of the encyclopedia.

- (F) amount
- (G) book
- (H) measurement
- (J) large

5. His grades have <u>improved</u>.

- (A) gotten better
- (B) gotten worse
- (C) fixed
- (D) painted

6. Tara's <u>excuse</u> was a good one.

- (F) dismiss
- (G) forgive
- (H) explanation
- (J) forgotten

The meaning of the sentence will give you a clue about which answer to choose.

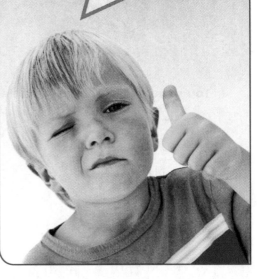

Chapter 1: Vocabulary

Words in Context

Directions: Look at each underlined phrase in the passage. Use the words around it to decide what it means. Then, answer the questions.

A Boomerang

Have you ever thrown a boomerang to see if it would spin back to you?

Boomerangs are <u>flat, curved objects that can be thrown</u> for fun or as a sport. There are two kinds of boomerangs—returning and nonreturning. A returning boomerang is made to <u>spin through the air in a curve and return</u> to the thrower. It is used mostly for fun or as a sport. The cave dwellers made nonreturning boomerangs. These boomerangs were <u>thrown in a straight path</u>. They were valuable hunting weapons because they could spin through the air and hit a target with great force.

Boomerangs were considered to be so important that they were often <u>decorated and used in ceremonies</u>.

1. **To what does <u>flat, curved objects that can be thrown</u> refer?**

   (A) cave dwellers

   (B) scientists

   (C) boomerangs

   (D) sport

2. **To what does <u>spin through the air in a curve and return</u> refer?**

   (F) fun or sport

   (G) a straight path

   (H) a nonreturning boomerang

   (J) a returning boomerang

3. **To what does <u>thrown in a straight path</u> refer?**

   (A) a nonreturning boomerang

   (B) a returning boomerang

   (C) cave dwellers

   (D) hunting weapons

4. **To what does <u>decorated and used in ceremonies</u> refer?**

   (F) boomerangs

   (G) important

   (H) stick

   (J) stone

Words in Context

Directions: Look at each underlined phrase in the passages. Use the words around it to decide what it means. Then, answer the questions.

A Microscope

Have you ever looked into a microscope? A microscope is an <u>instrument</u> that helps us see very small things by <u>magnifying</u> them. Scientists and doctors can use microscopes to study parts of the body, such as blood and skin cells. They can also study germs, tiny plants, and tiny animals.

1. In this passage, what does the word *instrument* mean?

(A) a tool

(B) a drum

(C) an office

(D) a paper

2. In this passage, what does the word *magnifying* mean?

(F) making them smaller

(G) making them larger

(H) making them red

(J) making them disappear

Paper Bowls

Making a papier-mâché bowl is a fun and simple craft. You need only a few <u>materials</u> and a bit of patience. Begin by cutting up pieces of tissue paper. Next, cover a small bowl with plastic wrap. Then, make a <u>solution</u> of water and flour. It should be thin enough to be easily spread with a paintbrush. Paint the bowl with the glue you made. Add a layer of tissue paper pieces. Then, add another layer of glue and tissue. Repeat this until you have five or six layers. Let the tissue dry overnight. The next day, you will have a papier-mâché bowl!

3. In this passage, what does the word *materials* mean?

(A) minutes

(B) items

(C) dollars

(D) suggestions

4. In this passage, what does the word *solution* mean?

(F) mixture

(G) mess

(H) juice

(J) problem

Sample Test 1: Vocabulary

Directions: Read each item. Choose the answer that means the same, or about the same, as the underlined word.

Example

<u>extremely</u> windy

(A) slightly

(B) somewhat

(C) often

(D) very

Answer: (D)

---

1. a <u>preferred</u> subject

(A) private

(B) known

(C) happy

(D) chosen

2. a <u>major</u> holiday

(F) different

(G) past

(H) big

(J) rewarded

3. a <u>soiled</u> shirt

(A) dirty

(B) clean

(C) used

(D) brand-new

4. leading <u>onward</u>

(F) down

(G) forward

(H) back

(J) aside

5. a <u>comfy</u> chair

(A) wooden

(B) folding

(C) hard

(D) cozy

6. a <u>salary</u> raise

(F) winning

(G) pay

(H) barn

(J) new

7. a <u>terrified</u> rabbit

(A) scared

(B) angry

(C) sad

(D) hungry

8. an important <u>test</u>

(F) paper

(G) contest

(H) exam

(J) unit

GO

Name _____   Date _____

Sample Test 1: Vocabulary

Directions: Read each item. Choose the answer that means the opposite of the underlined word.

9. Harriet Tubman <u>won</u> her freedom.
- (A) lost
- (B) pay
- (C) liberty
- (D) prize

10. The <u>grimy</u> cat stretched.
- (F) scared
- (G) small
- (H) happy
- (J) spotless

11. I find yard work <u>tiring</u>.
- (A) simple
- (B) energizing
- (C) hard
- (D) silly

12. Who will read the <u>brief</u> poem?
- (F) short
- (G) funny
- (H) tiny
- (J) long

Directions: For each item, choose the best word to fill in the blank.

13. The bus was more _____ than usual.
- (A) cost
- (B) crowded
- (C) hungry
- (D) walk

14. Don't forget to _____ your letter.
- (F) mail
- (G) small
- (H) happy
- (J) male

15. We can't sit in the _____ seats.
- (A) second
- (B) difficult
- (C) reserved
- (D) under

16. I think that Jeff is a _____ person.
- (F) third
- (G) basement
- (H) underneath
- (J) friendly

STOP

Purpose for Reading

Directions: Read the passage, and answer the questions.

Lunch Guests

It was a sunny spring day. Kaye and her friend, Tasha, were walking in the woods. As they walked, they noticed many squirrels ahead of them running in the same direction.

"Let's follow them and see where they are going," said Tasha.

"Great idea!" exclaimed Kaye, and the two girls raced ahead.

Soon, they came to a large clearing in the forest. There were hundreds and hundreds of squirrels—more squirrels than either girl had ever seen. As they stared in amazement at the scene before them, a plump gray squirrel with a fluffy tail skittered over to them and said politely, "Would you care to join us for lunch?"

Tasha and Kaye were stunned into silence. After a moment, they looked at each other, shrugged, and said, "Why not?" They both liked nuts.

1. The purpose of this passage is to _____.

Ⓐ entertain the reader

Ⓑ alarm the reader

Ⓒ inform the reader

Ⓓ challenge the reader

2. Explain why you chose your answer to question 1.

_____

_____

_____

_____

_____

_____

_____

Purpose for Reading

Directions: Read the passage, and answer the questions.

Quicksand

Stories of people and animals sinking into quicksand have been told for hundreds of years. Although some of the stories may be true, it helps to understand what quicksand really is.

Quicksand is a deep bed of light, loose sand that is full of water. On the surface, it looks much like regular sand, but it is really very different. Regular sand is packed firmly and can be walked on. Because quicksand is loose and full of water, it cannot support much weight. Quicksand usually develops around rivers and lakes. Water collects in the sand and does not drain away. It continues to collect until the sand becomes soft.

Although some objects can float in quicksand, it cannot support the heavy weight of an animal or a person.

1. The purpose of this passage is to _____.

(A) entertain the reader

(B) alarm the reader

(C) inform the reader

(D) challenge the reader

2. Explain why you chose your answer to question 1.

_____

_____

_____

_____

_____

_____

_____

Main Idea

Directions: Read each passage. Answer the questions that follow.

> **Example**
>
> At 5:00 P.M., we were called to the home of a Mr. and Mrs. Bear. They found that the lock on their front door had been forced open. Food had been stolen, and a chair was broken. Baby Bear then went upstairs and found someone asleep in his bed.
>
> **What is the main idea of this paragraph?**
>
> (A) Someone broke a lock.
>
> (B) Someone stole some food.
>
> (C) Mr. and Mrs. Bear's house was broken into.
>
> (D) Baby Bear found his bed.
>
> Answer: (C)

> You can look back at the passage to find an answer, but don't keep rereading the story.

Pioneer Diary

Today, we left our home in dear Ohio forever. Soon, we will be a thousand miles away. The distance is too great for us ever to return. Oh, how Grandmother cried as we said goodbye! Uncle Dan and Aunt Martha have bought our farm, so it is no longer our home. All we have now is what is here in our wagon.

When we drove past the woods at the edge of our fields, Papa said to me, "Ellen, take a good look at those trees. It will be many years before we see big trees like that again. We will have to plant trees on the prairie." I felt like crying, just like Grandmother, but I wanted to show Papa that I could be brave.

1. What is the main idea of this story?

(A) Ellen feels like crying.

(B) Ellen wants to be brave.

(C) Ellen and her father are moving to the prairie.

(D) Ellen's father has sold his farm.

2. How do you know where Ellen is moving?

(F) Her grandmother cries.

(G) Her father says that they will have to plant trees on the prairie.

(H) Her father has packed a wagon.

(J) Ellen is keeping a diary.

Name _____   Date _____

Main Idea

Directions: Read the passage, and answer the questions that follow.

A Bumpy Ride

When we first climbed into the car and strapped on our safety belts, I wasn't very nervous. I was sitting right next to my big brother, and he had done this many times before. As we started to climb the hill, however, I could feel my heart jump into my throat.

"Brian?" I asked nervously. "Is this supposed to be so noisy?"

"Sure, Matthew," Brian answered. "It always does that."

A minute later, we were going so fast down the hill that I didn't have time to think. With a twist, a loop, and a bunch of fast turns, everyone on board screamed in delight. No wonder this was one of the most popular rides in the park. By the time the car pulled into the station and we got off the ride, I was ready to do it again!

Cover the answer choices, and read the question. Think about your answer before you look at the choices.

Then, choose the option that is closest to your answer.

1. What is the main idea of this story?

(A) A big brother tries to frighten his little brother.

(B) A roller coaster breaks down with two brothers onboard.

(C) Matthew takes his first ride on a popular roller coaster.

(D) Passengers have to wear safety belts on roller coasters.

2. How do you know that Matthew enjoys the ride?

(F) He asks his brother if it is supposed to be noisy.

(G) It is one of the most popular rides in the park.

(H) Everyone screams on the ride.

(J) He wants to do it again.

Chapter 2: Reading Comprehension

Recalling Details

Directions: Read the passage, and answer the questions that follow.

Example

Emily Ann wears a long blue dress, a blue bonnet, and a shawl. Her head is made of china, and her shoes are real leather. Emily Ann has lived with the same family for almost two hundred years. But her new owner, Betty, is forgetful. Yesterday, she left Emily Ann in the park.

Which detail tells you that Emily Ann is a doll?

(A) Her shoes are made of leather.

(B) She wears a shawl.

(C) Her head is made of china.

(D) She wears a long blue dress.

Answer: C

The Perfect Party

Ian turned on his computer and started searching the Internet for ideas. This year, he wanted to give the best Fourth of July party ever. It was Ian's favorite holiday because it was also his birthday. Ian was looking for some ideas for games and prizes. He wanted recipes for red, white, and blue food. He also needed ideas for signs and decorations. When Ian saw a Web site called *Perfect Parties for Patriots*, he knew he had found exactly the right place to start his party planning.

1. Why is the Fourth of July Ian's favorite holiday?

(A) The Fourth of July is Ian's birthday.

(B) The Fourth of July is a great day for games and prizes.

(C) Red, white, and blue are his favorite colors.

(D) Ian is a patriot who loves his country.

2. Which of the following things did Ian not look for on the Internet?

(F) ideas for games and prizes

(G) recipes for red, white, and blue food

(H) ideas for decorations

(J) places to see firework displays

Name _____ Date _____

Recalling Details

Directions: Read the passage, and answer the questions that follow.

New Year's Traditions

Brazil: Most people in Brazil wear white clothes on New Year's Eve. They do this to bring them good luck and peace for the following year. If they live near the beach, they will jump seven waves and throw flowers into the sea while making a wish. This is believed to bring good luck and fortune.

China: The Chinese celebrate the new year in late January or early February. They eat dumplings on New Year's Eve for good luck. They also hang paper cuttings. They hope this will scare away evil spirits and bring them good luck for the new year.

Spain: One tradition is to eat 12 grapes at midnight. Spaniards eat one grape each time the clock chimes. This tradition began after a big grape harvest. The king of Spain decided to give grapes to everyone to eat on New Year's Eve.

United States: There are many different traditions in the United States. Some people in the South eat black-eyed peas and turnip greens on New Year's Day. The peas represent copper, and the turnip greens represent dollars. This is believed to bring good luck and wealth in the new year.

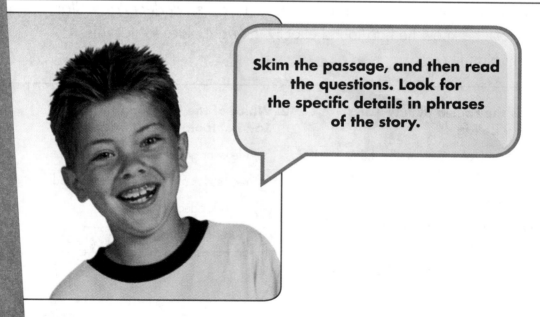

Skim the passage, and then read the questions. Look for the specific details in phrases of the story.

Recalling Details

Directions: Answer the questions about the passage on page 26.

1. **In what country do people eat 12 grapes at midnight on New Year's Eve?**

   (A) Brazil

   (B) China

   (C) Spain

   (D) United States

2. **If you live in Brazil, what color would you wear on New Year's Eve?**

   (F) white

   (G) red

   (H) blue

   (J) green

3. **Which country celebrates the new year in late January or early February?**

   (A) Brazil

   (B) China

   (C) Spain

   (D) United States

4. **What do black-eyed peas and turnip greens represent in the United States?**

   (F) gold and silver

   (G) coal and money

   (H) copper and dollars

   (J) wealth and good fortune

5. **If you celebrated the New Year in China, what would you eat for good luck?**

   (A) dumplings

   (B) beans

   (C) peas

   (D) grapes

6. **What do jumping seven waves and throwing flowers into the ocean represent in Brazil?**

   (F) gold

   (G) copper and dollars

   (H) peace

   (J) good luck and fortune

Recalling Details

Directions: Read the passage, and answer the questions that follow.

Wonderful Webs

Different types of spiders make different kinds of webs from the silk they spin. Tangled webs are made by house spiders and black widow spiders. These webs of tangled silk are used to trap insects for food in the same way that a fishnet traps fish. Sheet webs, made by platform spiders, are found in tall grass or in the branches of trees. When hunting, the platform spider hides under the sheet waiting for prey. Then, it pulls its catch through the webbing. The triangle spider makes a web shaped like its name. The sticky strands of this web catch insects that land on the surface.

1. What kind of web does a triangle spider weave?

(A) a pattern of circles

(B) a tangled-silk web

(C) a sticky, triangle-shaped web

(D) a messy cobweb

2. What is the purpose of a sheet web?

(F) to trap insects on the sticky surface

(G) to confuse insects and make them dizzy

(H) to serve as a place for the platform spider to hide

(J) to serve as a net to trap insects for food

3. Which of these is a fact about spiders?

(A) Platform spiders are smarter than other spiders.

(B) All webs work in the same way.

(C) Most webs are woven in a pattern of circles.

(D) Webs are used by spiders as a means of getting food.

4. Which of these is not a term used when describing spiders?

(F) spin

(G) web

(H) wings

(J) hunt

5. What conclusion can you draw from this passage?

_____

_____

_____

_____

_____

_____

_____

Making Inferences

Directions: Read each selection, and answer the questions that follow.

Example

One night in the woods, I saw a bright white spaceship under some trees. I was scared, but I tried to be brave. I was afraid the aliens might take me away to their planet. Suddenly, the spaceship opened and my friend Nadia got out. The spaceship was not a ship at all. It was just her family's camper!

Why do you think the author thought the camper was a spaceship?

(A) The author has seen many spaceships.

(B) The author has a good imagination.

(C) Nadia was playing a trick on the author.

(D) The author is an alien.   Answer: (B)

The Hitchhiker

I need to go across the street,
But I'm too tired. I have eight sore feet!
I'll climb up on this person's shoe.
I'll spin a safety belt or two.
Hey! Just a minute! It's time to stop.
Please let me off at this nice shop.
Just my luck! I picked someone,
Who doesn't walk—who'd rather run!

> If a question confuses you, try asking yourself the same question another way.

1. Who is the speaker in this poem?

(A) an older woman

(B) a dog

(C) a fly

(D) a spider

2. What clue tells you about the speaker's identity?

(F) tired

(G) needs to go across the street

(H) going shopping

(J) eight feet

Name _____   Date _____

Making Inferences

Directions: Read the passage. Answer the questions on the following page.

The Contest

Tat and Lin loved to enter contests. It did not matter what the prize was. Once, they wrote a poem for a magazine contest. They won a free copy of the magazine. Another time, they guessed how many marbles were in a glass jar. They got to take all the marbles home with them.

One morning, Tat was reading the Crunchy Munchies cereal box as he ate his breakfast. "Lin," he said. "Here's another contest! The first-place winner gets a bike. Second prize is a tent."

"Those are great prizes," said Lin. "How do we enter?" The box said that the boys had to fill out a box top with their names and address. The more box tops they filled out, the better their chances for winning the drawing. Tat and Lin started eating Crunchy Munchies every morning. They also asked everyone they knew for cereal box tops.

By the end of four weeks, Tat and Lin had 16 box tops to send in for the drawing. "I'm glad that's over," said Tat. "If I had to look at another box of that stuff, I don't know what I'd do."

A few weeks passed. One day, the boys got a letter in the mail. "Hooray! We've won third prize in the Crunchy Munchies contest!" Lin exclaimed. "I didn't even know there was a third prize."

Tat took the letter and started to read. His smile disappeared. "Oh, no!" he cried. "Third prize is a year's supply of Crunchy Munchies!"

Stay with your first choice for an answer. You are probably right!

Change your answer only if you are sure about your choice.

Making Inferences

Directions: Answer the questions based on the story on page 30.

1. What is this story about?

(A) two teachers who love cereal

(B) two cereal makers who love contests

(C) two sisters who play marbles

(D) two brothers who love contests

2. How do the boys find out about the Crunchy Munchies contest?

(F) from a letter in the mail

(G) from the back of a cereal box

(H) from their mother

(J) from their teacher

3. What is the problem in this story?

(A) Tat and Lin can't figure out how to enter the contest.

(B) Tat and Lin eat so much cereal that they can't stand it anymore.

(C) Tat and Lin don't collect enough box tops to win.

(D) Tat and Lin argue about who will get the prize.

4. What do you think Crunchy Munchies is like?

(F) smooth like pudding

(G) crisp and sweet

(H) cooked cereal, like oatmeal

(J) salty, like crackers

5. Why do you think the boys did not try to find out about the third prize before they entered the contest?

(A) because the third prize was added later

(B) because they thought they would win first prize

(C) because they forgot to write and find out

(D) because the prizes in contests didn't really matter to them

6. The next thing that Tat and Lin might do is

(F) find someone to whom they can give the cereal.

(G) enter another Crunchy Munchies contest.

(H) give up contests altogether.

(J) have a fight over who gets the cereal.

Fact and Opinion

Directions: Read the passage, and answer the questions that follow.

Example

It had snowed all night. "Hurray!" said Diego. "No school today! Snowstorms are the greatest!"

"Not only do I have to go to work," said Mom glumly, "but I also have to shovel snow."

Candy barked. She loved to play in the snow. She was as happy as Diego.

Which one of these statements is an opinion?

Ⓐ Mom had to shovel snow.

Ⓑ It had snowed all night.

Ⓒ Snowstorms are the greatest.

Ⓓ The dog was happy.   Answer: C

History Lesson

The students looked at the Web site, which told about the first Thanksgiving. "I think the Pilgrims were very brave," said Chad.

"When they came to Massachusetts, there were no other settlers from Europe," Keisha said. "I bet they probably felt lonely here."

"Their first year was a difficult one," Mr. Perez added. "Many of the Pilgrims became ill."

"I think I would have wanted to go home!" said Ang. "I would have felt that even boarding the *Mayflower* was a big mistake!"

---

1. What opinion did Keisha express?

Ⓐ The Pilgrims were the only European settlers in Massachusetts.

Ⓑ The Pilgrims had a difficult first year.

Ⓒ The Pilgrims wanted to go home.

Ⓓ The Pilgrims probably felt lonely.

2. Which character expressed only facts?

Ⓕ Chad

Ⓖ Keisha

Ⓗ Mr. Perez

Ⓙ Ang

Fact and Opinion

Directions: For each item, choose the sentence that is a fact.

1. (A) The Lions lost the game on Saturday.
   (B) They should have won.
   (C) If Miles had played, the Lions would have won.
   (D) We didn't practice hard enough this week.

2. (F) Fiction books are the most interesting.
   (G) Our library is the biggest in the city.
   (H) You will love the books on my reading list.
   (J) This summer, I will read more books than Erika.

3. (A) Cats make better pets than dogs.
   (B) You do not have to walk a cat.
   (C) Dogs are messier than cats.
   (D) A cat is a better companion.

4. (F) My sister should practice the piano more often.
   (G) She has a lot of talent.
   (H) She needs to spend less time on the computer.
   (J) My sister takes piano lesson on Fridays.

Are you hunting for opinions?

Be on the lookout for words like *believe*, *feel*, and *think*.

Directions: For each item, choose the sentence that is an opinion.

5. (A) Paul Revere was born in Boston.
   (B) He was a silversmith.
   (C) Paul Revere carried messages on horseback.
   (D) Revere is the most important figure in American history.

6. (F) Nuts and dried fruit make the best snack.
   (G) Nuts are a good source of protein.
   (H) Dried fruit has lots of fiber.
   (J) Junk foods have little nutrition.

7. (A) Many types of animals have become extinct.
   (B) Others are on the endangered list.
   (C) It is our job to help save them.
   (D) There are lots of groups working to do this.

8. (F) *Bridge to Terabithia* is a book by Katherine Paterson.
   (G) It has been made into a movie.
   (H) We read it last fall.
   (J) The book is better than the movie.

Story Elements

Directions: Read the passage, and answer the questions that follow.

The Runner

Alanna loved to run. She ran to school, and she ran home. She ran to the library and to her friends' houses. One day, she ran downstairs and said, "I think I'll train for the marathon this summer to raise money for the homeless shelter." She knew that the winner would get a trophy and $1,000 for the shelter.

Alanna started to train for the marathon. She bought a new pair of running shoes. She ran on the track and on the sidewalks. After a month, her knees started to hurt. The pain got worse, and her mother took Alanna to the doctor. "You have runner's knees," said the doctor. "You have done too much running without warming up. You'll have to do some exercises to strengthen your knees."

Alanna had to slow down for a couple of weeks. As she exercised, her pain decreased. Soon, she was able to run again. At the end of August, Alanna's friends stood cheering as she broke the tape at the finish line.

1. **What word best describes Alanna?**

   (A) smart

   (B) athletic

   (C) stubborn

   (D) musical

2. **What is the setting at the end of the story?**

   (F) Alanna's home

   (G) the doctor's office

   (H) the marathon

   (J) Alanna's school

3. **What is the problem in the story?**

   (A) Alanna loses the marathon.

   (B) Alanna runs on the sidewalk and ruins her shoes.

   (C) Alanna runs in too many places and hurts her knees.

   (D) Alanna runs without warming up and gets runner's knees.

Story Elements

Directions: Read the short story. Then, answer each question below.

A Friend's Visit

Juan looked at the clock. He paced across the floor. His best friend, Bill, was coming to visit for the first time in six months. Bill had moved very far away. Juan wondered if they would still feel like good friends.

The doorbell rang, and Juan raced to answer it. Bill looked a bit unsure. Juan smiled and started talking just as they always had when they lived near one another. He made Bill feel comfortable. As the day went on, it felt like old times.

Pay attention to the way a character is acting. This can give you clues about how the character is feeling.

1. Who are the main characters in this story?

_____

_____

2. Where does the story take place?

_____

_____

3. When does the story take place? Now? In the past? In the future?

_____

4. What problem does Juan have?

_____

_____

_____

_____

_____

5. What clues in the story helped you to understand how Juan is feeling?

_____

_____

_____

6. How does Juan try to solve his problems?

_____

_____

_____

Fiction

Directions: Read the story, and answer the questions on the following page.

Wendy, Lost and Found

Wendy was scared. For the second time in her young life, she was lost. When the branch fell on the fence and her small house, she had barely escaped. She had leaped across the fallen fence into the woods. Now, the rain poured down and the wind howled. The little woodchuck shivered under a big oak tree. She did not know what to do.

When Wendy was a baby, her mother had died. She had been alone in the woods then, too. She could not find enough food. Then, she hurt her paw. All day, she scratched at a small hole in the ground, trying to make a <u>burrow</u>. Every night, she was hungry.

One day, Rita found her. Rita had knelt down by Wendy's shallow burrow and set down an apple. Wendy limped out slowly and took the apple. It was the best thing she had ever tasted. Rita took the baby woodchuck to the wildlife center. Wendy had lived there ever since. Most of the animals at the center were orphans. Rita taught them how to live in the wild and then let them go when they were ready. But Wendy's paw did not heal well, and Rita knew that Wendy would never go back to the wild. So, Rita made Wendy a house and a pen. Wendy even had a job—she visited schools with Rita so that students could learn all about woodchucks.

Now, the storm had ruined Wendy's house. She did not know how to find Rita. At dawn, the rain ended. Wendy limped down to a big stream and sniffed the air. Maybe the center was across the stream. Wendy jumped onto a rock and then hopped to another one. She landed on her bad paw and fell into the fast-moving water. The little woodchuck struggled to keep her nose above water. The current had tossed her against a tangle of branches. Wendy held on with all her might.

"There she is!" Wendy heard Rita's voice. Rita and Ben, another worker from the wildlife center, were across the stream. Rita waded out to the branches, lifted Wendy up, and wrapped her in a blanket. Wendy purred her thanks. By the time Ben and Rita got into the van to go back to the center, Wendy was fast asleep.

Fiction

Directions: Answer the questions based on the story on page 36.

1. What genre is this passage?

Ⓐ biography

Ⓑ nonfiction

Ⓒ fiction

Ⓓ poetry

Do you see any easy questions? Answer those first. Then, move on to the others.

2. This passage is mostly about _____.

Ⓕ a wildlife center worker

Ⓖ a woodchuck who lives at a wildlife center

Ⓗ a woodchuck who can do tricks

Ⓙ a woodchuck who learns how to swim

3. How does the passage start?

Ⓐ with Wendy's life as a baby

Ⓑ in the middle of the storm

Ⓒ with Wendy's visit to school

Ⓓ when Wendy is in the stream

4. What are the settings for this passage?

Ⓕ the woods and the wildlife center

Ⓖ the school and the stream

Ⓗ the school and the woods

Ⓙ the wildlife center and Rita's house

5. How did Wendy get out of the house that Rita built for her?

Ⓐ Rita forgot to lock the door.

Ⓑ Ben let her out.

Ⓒ A branch fell on the house.

Ⓓ The stream flooded her house.

6. What is a _burrow_?

Ⓕ an animal's home in the ground

Ⓖ a type of food

Ⓗ a small wooden house

Ⓙ a group of woodchucks

Name _____   Date _____

Fiction

Directions: Read the story. Then, answer the questions on the following page.

Danny's Day on the Trail

Today was the day I had been dreading—our class nature hike. My mother could barely drag me out of bed. I hate being outdoors. I'd rather be in my room, zapping alien spaceships. When I'm outside, I always feel clumsy. Plus, I always get poison ivy, even if I'm miles away from the plants!

On the bus, Mr. Evans handed out lists for us to fill in during our nature hike. We were supposed to write down how many animals we spotted and which rocks and leaves we could find. As if the hike itself wasn't bad enough! I lost my canteen right away. It rolled down a cliff and bounced into the river. Then, I ripped my t-shirt on a bush that had huge thorns. I did manage to find a couple of the rocks on our list, but only because I tripped on them. I'm sure there wasn't a single animal anywhere on the trail. Of course, I did fall down a lot, so maybe I scared them all away.

By the time we got back to the bus, I was hot, dirty, and tired. I was so glad to get back home that I nearly hugged my computer. But by bedtime, it was clear that somehow I had gotten poison ivy again. I was covered with it!

Look for key words in the story and the questions to help you find the right answers.

Fiction

Directions: Answer the questions about the story on page 38.

1. **What word best describes Danny's day?**

   Ⓐ enjoyable

   Ⓑ scary

   Ⓒ unhappy

   Ⓓ interesting

2. **What happened to Danny's canteen on the hike?**

   Ⓕ It broke on a rock on the trail.

   Ⓖ It rolled down a cliff and got lost in the woods.

   Ⓗ It rolled down a cliff and got lost in the river.

   Ⓙ It got left behind because Danny forgot it.

3. **What do you think is Danny's hobby?**

   Ⓐ playing computer games

   Ⓑ bird watching

   Ⓒ sleeping

   Ⓓ hiking

4. **Which of these is an opinion?**

   Ⓕ Mr. Evans handed out lists we were supposed to fill in.

   Ⓖ I fell down a lot.

   Ⓗ It's so much more interesting playing computer games.

   Ⓙ I had poison ivy again!

5. **Choose the correct order of the settings for this story.**

   Ⓐ the bus, the nature trail, the bus, Danny's home

   Ⓑ Danny's home, the nature trail, the bus

   Ⓒ the bus, the nature trail, the bus, Danny's classroom

   Ⓓ Danny's home, the bus, the nature trail, the bus, Danny's home

6. **The boxes show some things that happened in the story. What belongs in Box 2?**

Danny gets a list on the bus.	Box 2	Danny gets back on the bus.

   Ⓕ Danny doesn't want to get out of bed.

   Ⓖ Danny rips his t-shirt on a thorn.

   Ⓗ Danny finds out he has poison ivy.

   Ⓙ Danny nearly hugs his computer.

7. **Why do you think the author has Danny talk about his problems on the trail?**

   Ⓐ to make him seem brave

   Ⓑ to add humor to the story

   Ⓒ to show how much he loves hiking

   Ⓓ to show that he talked too much

Name _____   Date _____

Fiction

Directions: Read the passage, and answer the questions that follow.

Black Beauty
paraphrased from *Black Beauty*
by Anna Sewell

One day, when there was a good deal of kicking in the meadow, my mother whinnied to me to come to her.

"I wish you to pay attention to what I am about to say. The colts who live here are very good colts, but they are cart-horse colts, and of course, they have not learned manners. You have been <u>well-bred</u> and <u>wellborn</u>; your father has a great name in these parts. Your grandfather won the cup two years in a row at the Newmarket Races; your grandmother had the sweetest temper of any horse I have ever known. I think you have never seen me kick or bite. I hope you will grow up gentle and good and never follow bad ways. Do your work with good will, lift your legs up high when you trot, and never kick or bite, even in play."

In this passage, the *cup* is a kind of horse race. *Temper* is the personality of the horse.

1. Which of the following is an opinion?

(A) Your grandfather won the cup two years in a row at the Newmarket Races.

(B) My mother whinnied to me to come to her.

(C) The colts who live here are very good colts.

(D) None of the above

2. Which word best describes the attitude of Black Beauty's mother?

(F) proud

(G) angry

(H) sad

(J) carefree

3. In your own words, write what you think *well-bred* and *wellborn* means.

_____

_____

_____

_____

_____

Fiction

Directions: Read the passage, and answer the questions that follow.

Why the Sun and the Moon Live in the Sky
a Ghana folktale

Many, many years ago, the Sun and the Moon lived together on Earth. Water was their best friend, and they often came to see him. But Water never went to see the Sun and the Moon in their house. The Sun asked Water why he didn't visit. Water answered that he had too many friends and was afraid there would be no place for them in his house.

So, the Sun built a very big house and then asked Water to come to him. Water came with all the fish and water animals. Soon, Water was up to the Sun's head and came higher and higher with all the fish and water animals. At last, Water was so high in the house that the Sun and the Moon went to the roof and sat there. Water soon came up onto the roof. What could the Sun and the Moon do? Where could they sit? They went up to the sky. They liked the place and began to live there.

1. This folktale explains _____.

(A) why the Sun and the Moon live with Water

(B) why the Sun and the Moon live in the sky

(C) why Water does not like the Sun and the Moon

(D) why the Sun built a very small house

2. Why didn't Water want to visit the Sun and the Moon in their house?

(F) Their house was too big.

(G) He was worried there wouldn't be enough room for all his friends.

(H) He did not get along with the Moon.

(J) He knew they could not swim.

3. Which of the following happened first?

(A) The Sun and the Moon began to live in the sky.

(B) Water came to visit the Sun and the Moon in their house.

(C) Water came up onto the roof.

(D) The Sun built a big house.

4. This selection is a piece of fiction about the Sun and the Moon. How would a nonfiction selection about the sun and the moon be different?

_____

_____

_____

_____

Fiction

Directions: Read the passage, and answer the questions that follow.

Summer Jam

The summer I was eight, my grandmother taught me how to make strawberry jam. We picked the berries from a neighbor's field. Grandma promised to bring them a few jars of jam in return. We spent an hour hunched over the plants in the morning sun. Our buckets were filled to the brim with the plump red fruit. My fingers were stained red, and so was my mouth. Grandma laughed. "That's a sign of good, sweet berries!" she said.

When we got home, we carefully rinsed the berries and chopped them. Grandma added them to her big silver pot, and I poured in the sugar. As they cooked, the kitchen was filled with the sweetest smell!

Grandma taught me how to can the jam. We wanted it to last through the winter. "There's nothing like a little taste of summer on a snowy day," she said.

Grandma and I brought a jar of our jam to the county fair the next weekend. When we stopped by the booth after lunch, there was a blue ribbon on our jar. First place! Ever since that day, Grandma has called her jam *blue-ribbon preserves*.

1. What did Grandma give the neighbors in return for their berries?

(A) some money

(B) a few jars of jam

(C) a blue ribbon

(D) some sugar

2. What does *hunched* mean?

(F) bent

(G) squeezed

(H) standing

(J) walking

3. Why was there a blue ribbon on the jar of jam?

(A) Grandma put the ribbon there.

(B) The jam had gone bad.

(C) It had won first prize.

(D) It was blueberry jam.

4. Which of the following is an opinion?

(F) Grandma taught me how to can the jam.

(G) We spent an hour hunched over the plants in the morning sun.

(H) We picked the berries from a neighbor's field.

(J) The kitchen was filled with the sweetest smell!

Nonfiction

Directions: Read the passage, and answer the questions that follow.

A Busy Morning

The finches are the first to arrive at the feeder. They chirp and take turns eating the seeds. Later, the doves join them. The doves almost never eat at feeders. Instead, they like to peck the seeds that have fallen to the ground. After they have eaten, they sometimes settle down near a plant in the garden to rest.

Another bird that eats on the ground is the junco. Juncos usually arrive in flocks of about 10. They are shy birds and fly away at the first sound or movement of a person in the yard. The sparrows fly to and from the feeder all morning long. They are lively birds that chirp, hop, chase each other, and go from the feeder to their home in the hedge and back again.

1. **Another title that shows the main idea of this passage is**

   (A) "My Favorite Bird."

   (B) "Juncos and Doves."

   (C) "Backyard Birds."

   (D) "Sparrows in the Hedge."

2. **Which birds like to eat on the ground?**

   (F) finches and doves

   (G) doves and sparrows

   (H) juncos and doves

   (J) finches and sparrows

3. **Which type of bird probably stays on the ground the longest?**

   (A) finch

   (B) dove

   (C) junco

   (D) sparrow

4. **Which statement is a fact from the passage?**

   (F) Juncos are the most beautiful birds in the backyard.

   (G) Doves eat seeds on the ground, not in the feeder.

   (H) Juncos usually arrive in flocks of about 20.

   (J) Juncos seem greedy about food compared to other birds.

Nonfiction

Directions: Read the passage, and answer the questions that follow.

Therapy Dogs

Therapy dogs can help patients get better after illnesses. The dogs' owners bring them into hospital rooms and let patients meet the animals. Dogs sometimes go right up to patients' beds. People in the hospital rooms can pet the dogs, brush them, and talk to them. Studies have shown that being with dogs and other animals is <u>therapeutic</u>. It can reduce stress, lower blood pressure, and help people heal faster.

Not every dog is a good choice for this important job. To be a therapy dog, a dog must have a calm, friendly <u>disposition</u>. Some therapy dog owners feel that their pets were born to help sick people get well again.

Not sure about an answer?

First, decide which choices you know are wrong. Then, skim the passage again to figure out which of the other choices is the correct answer.

1. What is the main idea of this passage?

(A) Therapy dogs like to be brushed.

(B) Therapy dogs are calm and friendly.

(C) Therapy dogs help patients get better after illnesses.

(D) Therapy dogs were born to visit hospitals.

2. The word *disposition* means

(F) work history.

(G) personality.

(H) intelligence.

(J) breed.

3. Which words help you figure out the meaning of *therapeutic*?

(A) "sometimes go right up to patients' beds"

(B) "reduce stress, lower blood pressure, and help people heal faster"

(C) "a calm, friendly disposition"

(D) "born to help sick people get well again"

4. Which of these would not describe a therapy dog?

(F) friendly

(G) nervous

(H) calm

(J) patient

Nonfiction

Directions: Read the selection. Then, answer the questions on the following page.

Making Clay Move

Beginning in about 1990, *claymation* became very popular. <u>Animators</u> have used clay animation to make several famous movies and TV commercials. However, claymation is not a new idea. In 1897, a claylike material called *plasticine* was invented. Moviemakers used plasticine to create clay animation films as early as 1908. Animators could use the plasticine models for scenes that could not be filmed in real life.

Here's how claymation works. First, an artist makes one or more clay models. Moviemakers pose each model and take a picture. Next, they move the model into a slightly different pose. Then, they take another picture. They continue the pattern of taking pictures, moving the model, and taking pictures again. Hundreds of pictures may make only a few seconds of film. The idea of using models and <u>stop-action photography</u> came from a French animator named George Melier. He once had a job as a magician and called his work *trick film*.

Today's animators use different kinds of clay. They can also use computers to speed up the claymation process. But the basic idea of clay animation has not changed in more than one hundred years!

If you have enough time, review both questions and answers. You might see something you missed!

Nonfiction

Directions: Answer the questions about the selection on page 45.

1. This selection is mostly about

(A) the history of claymation films.

(B) George Melier, a French magician.

(C) making models out of plasticine.

(D) today's animators and how they work.

2. What do you think *stop-action photography* is?

(F) making everyone stop while a photo is taken

(G) moving a model, taking the picture, then moving the model again

(H) using magic tricks to make the camera work

(J) a camera that stops after the picture is taken

3. Which of these choices is a fact?

(A) Claymation movies are funnier than live-action movies.

(B) Claymation movies are more interesting than other movies.

(C) Claymation movies weren't very good until the 1990s.

(D) Claymation movies were first made in 1908.

4. What is an *animator*?

(F) someone who works with actors

(G) someone who makes clay sculptures

(H) someone who invents clay materials

(J) someone who makes animated films

5. Who was George Melier?

(A) a filmmaker who became a magician

(B) a magician who became an animator

(C) a clay-model maker who liked to play tricks

(D) the inventor of plasticine

6. The author wrote this passage to

(F) entertain readers with funny stories of filmmaking.

(G) inform readers about the claymation process.

(H) make readers want to rent specific DVDs.

(J) tell the history of plasticine.

Nonfiction

Directions: Read the selection, and answer the questions that follow.

Cheetahs

Cheetahs are animals that have tawny fur coats with round black spots. They belong to the cat family, just like lions and cougars. However, cheetah babies are called *cubs*, not *kittens*. The cubs start following their mother on hunts when they are only six weeks old. When they are six months old, the cubs start learning from their mother how to hunt for themselves.

It is amazing that cheetahs in the wild can run up to 60 miles per hour. They are the fastest animals in the world. When cheetahs hunt, it is usually at night. They creep up on their prey. Then, with a single bound, the cheetah can catch an animal in a burst of speed. If it has to, a cheetah can run for over three miles at an average speed of 45 miles per hour.

Today, cheetahs are struggling to survive on land that was once good hunting ground. Today, it is being farmed. In Africa, Southwest Asia, and India, where the cheetahs live, farmers set traps for these animals. The cheetahs hunt cattle, and the farmers lose money when their livestock is killed. In the past 10 years, for example, farmers in Namibia have trapped and killed more than 7,000 cheetahs.

1. Which one of these statements is a fact?

(A) Cheetahs are the most beautiful animals in the world.

(B) Cheetahs should not be killed by farmers.

(C) Cheetahs are the fastest land animals in the world.

(D) Cheetahs would make great pets.

2. Where is the cheetah's habitat?

(F) Africa, China, and India

(G) Southwest Asia, Africa, and India

(H) Australia, Asia, and India

(J) Africa, Namibia, and India

Name _____   Date _____

Nonfiction

Directions: Answer the questions about the selection on page 47.

3. Why might someone think that baby cheetahs should be called *kittens* rather than *cubs*?

Ⓐ because *kitten* is the word for baby cat, and cheetahs belong to the cat family

Ⓑ because *kitten* is a word that describes small animals with spots and pointed ears

Ⓒ because *kitten* is a word used for all cute babies

Ⓓ because *kitten* is the term used for baby animals

4. How old are cheetah cubs when they learn to hunt for themselves?

Ⓕ one year old

Ⓖ six weeks old

Ⓗ six months old

Ⓙ six years old

5. Which statement is true?

Ⓐ Cheetahs can run up to 60 miles per hour.

Ⓑ Cheetahs have black fur with tawny spots.

Ⓒ Cheetahs make traps for their prey.

Ⓓ Cheetahs are being killed by farmers in the United States.

6. Which statement is false?

Ⓕ Cheetahs have more fun hunting than other animals.

Ⓖ Cheetahs surprise their prey with bursts of speed.

Ⓗ Cheetah mothers teach their cubs to hunt for themselves.

Ⓙ In the past 10 years, farmers in Namibia have killed more than 7,000 cheetahs.

7. What conclusion can you draw from the last paragraph of the passage?

_____

_____

_____

_____

Every part of a true sentence must be true!

Nonfiction

Directions: Read the selection, and answer the questions that follow.

Planet Temperatures

Scientists have looked at other planets in our solar system to see if they would be good places to live. One of the first problems is temperature. Earth's average temperature is about 58°F, which is the temperature on a brisk fall day. Our neighbor Venus is one planet closer to the sun than Earth, and much hotter. The average temperature on Venus is 867°F. This is mostly because of Venus's thick atmosphere, which traps the sun's heat so it cannot escape. The trapping of the atmosphere in this way is called the *greenhouse effect*. It is named for the way that hot air gets trapped inside a greenhouse and is kept warmer than the air outside. On the other hand, Earth's neighbor Mars is one planet further away from the sun. It is a little too cold for comfort on Mars. Its average temperature is −13°F, the temperature of a very cold winter day in Chicago.

1. **What is the *greenhouse effect*?**

   (A) air that is trapped by glass and cannot escape

   (B) air that is heated by the sun and then trapped by a planet's thick atmosphere

   (C) air that is heated by the sun and then orbits a planet and keeps it warm

   (D) air that travels from one planet to another

2. **Which of these might be an example of the greenhouse effect?**

   (F) a car on a summer's day with the air conditioning on

   (G) a parked car on a summer's day with the windows closed

   (H) a car on a summer's day that is traveling down the highway with the windows open

   (J) a parked car on a summer's day with all of the windows open

3. **After reading the passage, which of these statements do you think is probably true?**

   (A) The average temperature increases the closer a planet is to the sun.

   (B) The average temperature increases the closer a planet is to Earth.

   (C) The average temperature decreases the closer a planet is to the sun.

   (D) The average temperature increases the further a planet is from the sun.

4. **After reading the passage, which conclusion can you draw?**

   (F) With the proper shelter, it would be possible to live on Mars.

   (G) With the proper shelter, it would be possible to live on Venus.

   (H) Earth's average temperature is colder than Mars' average temperature.

   (J) Earth's average temperature is warmer than Venus's average temperature.

Name _____   Date _____

Nonfiction

Directions: Read the selection. Then, answer the questions on the following page.

The Voyage of the *Mayflower*

The Puritans came to America for religious freedom. In the early 1600s, most English people attended the Church of England. A group of people did not like the Church of England's services. This group became known as the *Puritans*. They were not treated well in England because of their beliefs.

A man named *William Bradford* decided to lead a group of Puritans to Holland. The Dutch people were kind to the Puritans. Still, the country never felt like home to the wandering group. They started to call themselves *Pilgrims*, which means *a group of people who go on a quest or journey because of their beliefs*. The group decided to travel to the New World and make their home there.

In September of 1620, a ship named the *Mayflower* set sail for America, carrying 35 Pilgrims and 67 hired craftspeople. They were heading for Virginia, but a storm blew the ship off course. The Mayflower landed hundreds of miles north, at what is now called *Cape Cod* in Massachusetts.

The Pilgrims had to make a decision. Should they sail down the coast to Virginia or try to build their settlement in this northern land? Some of the hired workers wanted to go to Virginia, as they had been promised. Some of the Pilgrims wanted to stay because they were tired and ill after their long trip. The Pilgrim leaders decided that everyone had to sign an agreement. This contract, called the *Mayflower Compact*, stated that for the good of the colony everyone had to obey the leaders and stay together to build a settlement.

The Pilgrims lived onboard the *Mayflower* until houses were built for them on the mainland. Many of the Pilgrims were not able to move into their new homes until the spring of 1621.

Nonfiction

Directions: Answer the questions about the selection on page 50.

1. Why did the Puritans decide to leave England?

(A) because it did not feel like home

(B) because the Puritans were not treated well in England

(C) because the Puritans wanted to settle in Massachusetts

(D) because the Puritans wanted to explore Holland

2. What is the meaning of the word *compact* in this passage?

(F) something small

(G) a powder holder

(H) a contract

(J) a will

3. What went wrong with the Pilgrims' plan to settle in Virginia?

(A) Their ship was blown off course to the north.

(B) Their ship was blown off course to the south.

(C) They decided to go back to Holland.

(D) They decided to sail to Massachusetts.

4. Why did the Puritans call themselves *Pilgrims*?

(F) because they were grim and unhappy

(G) because they were crossing an ocean

(H) because they were on a trip connected to their beliefs

(J) because they were sure they were in the right

5. Do you think that the Mayflower Compact was needed? Explain your answer.

_____

_____

_____

_____

_____

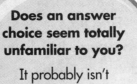

Does an answer choice seem totally unfamiliar to you?

It probably isn't the correct choice.

Name _____ Date _____

Nonfiction

Directions: Read the selection, and answer the questions that follow.

Changes in the Rainforest

Rainforests all over the world are being cleared, or cut down. They might be cleared for the trees. The wood from the trees is used in products such as furniture and paper. At other times, they are cleared for the land. The land is then used for growing crops or raising animals for food.

We have learned that there are problems with destroying the rainforests. One problem is erosion. When the trees are removed, the roots are no longer there to hold the soil in place. This causes the soil to erode, or wear away. Heavy equipment is used to cut down and move the logs to other places. Driving this equipment back and forth on the land also causes the soil to break down and wash away. Another problem is pollution. The heavy equipment creates air and water pollution. Fires used to burn down the trees cause air pollution.

Rainforests are home to millions of plants, animals, and insects. Researchers have found plants in the rainforest that can be used to make medicines. They are concerned that these plants will disappear before more discoveries are made. These natural resources could be used to prevent or heal diseases. This would be worth more than the lumber from the trees or the income from farming or ranching.

1. How does clearing rainforests affect pollution?

Ⓐ It decreases air and water pollution.

Ⓑ It increases air and water pollution.

Ⓒ It has no effect on pollution.

Ⓓ It helps to prevent pollution.

2. How is the land used after the trees are cleared from the rainforest?

Ⓕ It is used for farming.

Ⓖ It is used for ranching.

Ⓗ It is used for both farming and ranching.

Ⓙ The land is not used for other purposes.

3. How is the soil in the rainforest affected when trees are removed?

Ⓐ The soil erodes and washes away.

Ⓑ The soil builds up.

Ⓒ The amount of soil stays the same.

Ⓓ None of the above

4. Describe why we might not want to continue to clear the rainforests.

_____

_____

_____

_____

Chapter 2: Reading Comprehension

Identifying Literature Genres

Directions: Each of these passages is a different genre, or type of writing. Read the passages, and answer the questions on the following page.

The Great Ice Age

Long ago, the climate of Earth began to cool. As the temperature dropped, giant sheets of ice, called *glaciers*, moved across the land. As time went on, snow and ice covered many forests and grasslands.

Some plants and animals could not survive the changes in the climate. Other animals moved to warmer land. But some animals were able to adapt. They learned to live with the cold and snowy weather.

Finally, Earth's temperature began to rise. The ice and snow began to melt. Today, the land at the North and South Poles is a reminder of the Great Ice Age.

The Fox and the Grapes

One warm summer day, a fox was walking along. He noticed a bunch of grapes on a vine above him. Cool, juicy grapes would taste so good! The more he thought about it, the more the fox wanted those grapes.

He tried standing on his tiptoes. He tried jumping high in the air. He tried getting a running start before he jumped. But no matter what he tried, the fox could not reach the grapes.

As he angrily walked away, the fox muttered, "They were probably sour anyway!"

Moral: A person (or fox) sometimes pretends that he does not want something he cannot have.

Marie Curie

One of the greatest scientists of all time was Marie Curie. Marie was born in Poland in 1867. She studied at a university in Paris and lived in France for most of her adult life.

Marie and her husband, Pierre, studied radioactivity. She won the Nobel Prize in chemistry in 1911. Some medical advances are based on the work of the Curies. They include the X-ray and the use of radiation to treat cancer.

The Curies were both generous people. They were poor for most of their lives, but they did not keep the rights to any of their discoveries. They wanted everyone to benefit from their research.

Spring Garden

Trees tap at my window
And tell me to come
Out to the garden
Where the wind plays and hums.

Small green buds whisper
Secrets to me
Of spring coming soon
And of flowers yet to be.

Identifying Literature Genres

Directions: Answer the questions about the passages on page 53.

A **biography** tells the story of a real person's life. A **fable** has a moral, or lesson about how to act. **Nonfiction** includes facts or tells a true story. A **poem** often has rhyming words.

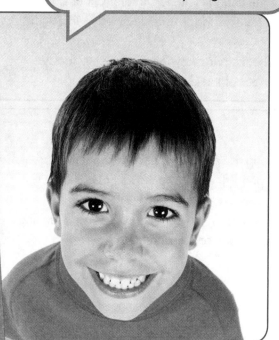

1. Which of the passages is a biography?

- (A) "The Great Ice Age"
- (B) "Marie Curie"
- (C) "The Fox and the Grapes"
- (D) "Spring Garden"

2. Which of the passages is a fable?

- (F) "The Great Ice Age"
- (G) "Marie Curie"
- (H) "The Fox and the Grapes"
- (J) "Spring Garden"

3. Which of the passages is nonfiction?

- (A) "The Great Ice Age"
- (B) "The Fox and the Grapes"
- (C) "Spring Garden"
- (D) None of the above

4. Which of the passages is a poem?

- (F) "The Great Ice Age"
- (G) "Marie Curie"
- (H) "The Fox and the Grapes"
- (J) "Spring Garden"

5. What genre, or type of writing, do you like the best? Explain your answer.

_____

_____

_____

_____

_____

_____

_____

Sample Test 2: Reading Comprehension 55

Directions: Read the selection, and answer the questions that follow.

The Castle at Yule

Wyn was excited. The Great Hall was almost ready for the Yule feast. Fresh straw had been spread on the stone floor, and the tables were set with bowls, spoons, and cups. Kitchen maids hurried to bring out the food for the first course. Pipers were practicing their best music. Wyn watched as the huge Yule log was rolled into the fireplace. It would burn there for the next 12 days and nights. "Soon the feasting will start," thought Wyn, "and even I, a simple page, will be able to eat my fill. Truly, this winter holiday is the best time of the whole year!"

1. This story is mostly about
- (A) a piper.
- (B) a kitchen maid.
- (C) a page.
- (D) the lord of the castle.

2. What is set on the tables?
- (F) bowls, knives, and forks
- (G) plates, spoons, and cups
- (H) bowls, spoons, and cups
- (J) knives, forks, and spoons

3. How long do you think Yule lasts?
- (A) one day
- (B) one night
- (C) 10 days and nights
- (D) 12 days and nights

4. What opinion does Wyn express?
- (F) The feasting will begin soon.
- (G) Yule is the best time of the year.
- (H) A page will be able to eat his fill.
- (J) The Great Hall was almost ready.

GO

Sample Test 2: Reading Comprehension

56

Directions: Read the following diary entries. Then, answer the questions.

April 27, 1856 We started West from Independence [Missouri] today. Pa has already made us lighten the wagon load. We have two oxen that are pulling it. We will be following the Oregon Trail. Pa says it will take us five to six months to reach Oregon.

May 4 We have settled into our routine. We are up at 5 and make camp for the night at 6 in the evening. By 9 o'clock, we are in bed—which, many times, is just sleeping on the ground. There's not much room in the wagon, so we walk most of the way. My little sister gets to ride more than the rest of us. Pa says we travel about 15 miles a day.

May 15 The weather was cold. Had trouble crossing the river, but both we and the wagon made it. There was plenty of wood for the fire and grass for the oxen. The number of buffalo we see along the Platte River is amazing. Made 11 miles today.

June 7 We arrived in Fort Laramie [Wyoming]. We've been traveling for six weeks. The Rocky Mountains are ahead of us. We bought some new supplies, but they were very expensive. We were able to post a letter to Grandpa and Grandma. I fear we shall never see them again, as I doubt we shall ever return East.

5. What do the diary entries describe?

- (A) a typical family vacation in the 1850s
- (B) a journey West along the Oregon Trail
- (C) life at a fort in the 1850s
- (D) the postal service in the 1850s

6. What form of transportation did this family use to travel along the trail?

- (F) They rode in a boat along the river.
- (G) They rode in a train that followed the trail.
- (H) They walked and rode in a wagon pulled by oxen.
- (J) They rode on horses.

7. How long did the typical journey from Missouri to Oregon take?

- (A) 5 to 6 months
- (B) 6 weeks
- (C) 4 months
- (D) 15 months

8. Which of the following resources would you use to find the locations of the places mentioned in the diary?

- (F) a dictionary
- (G) a collection of photos of the Old West
- (H) a map
- (J) a newspaper

STOP

Practice Test 1: Reading
Part 1: Vocabulary

Directions: Choose the answer that means the same, or about the same, as the underlined word.

1. a <u>fearless</u> dog

(A) careless

(B) energetic

(C) unafraid

(D) sincere

2. <u>solar</u> energy

(F) sun-powered

(G) sunburn

(H) sometimes

(J) powerful

3. an <u>ancient</u> castle

(A) strong

(B) bridge

(C) stone

(D) old

4. The train had only one <u>passenger</u>.

(F) ticket

(G) car

(H) rider

(J) conductor

Directions: Read each item. Choose the answer that means the opposite of the underlined word.

5. He decided to <u>continue</u>.

(A) stop

(B) go on

(C) roost

(D) sleep

6. The doctor <u>comforted</u> his patient.

(F) bothered

(G) cheered

(H) recognized

(J) calmed

7. She was a <u>mighty</u> warrior.

(A) great

(B) strong

(C) famous

(D) weak

GO

Practice Test 1: Reading
Part 1: Vocabulary

Directions: Read the two sentences. Choose the word that fits in the blank in both sentences.

8. I did not shed a _____ over my lost paper.
Dad will mend the _____ in my jacket.

- (F) tear
- (G) thread
- (H) break
- (J) banner

9. Mom broke a marathon _____ in the race.
I want to _____ my thoughts in a diary.

- (A) note
- (B) record
- (C) write
- (D) tape

10. Everyone's _____ on the field trip was great.
She wants to _____ the orchestra.

- (F) job
- (G) position
- (H) conduct
- (J) tape

11. Everyone in the class was _____.
She picked out a nice birthday _____.

- (A) quiet
- (B) present
- (C) comfortable
- (D) gift

Directions: Find the answer in which the underlined word is used in the same way as it is in the box.

12. The ⬜ field ⬜ is planted with corn.

- (F) The <u>field</u> of technology is always changing.
- (G) We can see deer in the <u>field</u> by our house.
- (H) Her <u>field</u> is nursing.
- (J) Our <u>field</u> trip is next Thursday.

13. The ⬜ general ⬜ idea was to weave a basket.

- (A) She is a <u>general</u> in the army.
- (B) The soldiers followed their <u>general</u> into battle.
- (C) I think that the <u>general</u> had the best idea.
- (D) No <u>general</u> study of history can cover everything.

14. She wants the same ⬜ type ⬜ of coat.

- (F) Akiko can <u>type</u> very fast.
- (G) Let me <u>type</u> up this report.
- (H) I like this <u>type</u> of cereal the best.
- (J) He has to <u>type</u> in new data all the time.

Practice Test 1: Reading
Part 1: Vocabulary

Directions: Read each item. Choose the answer that fits best in the blank.

15. Brave _____ circled the globe.

   (A) dogs

   (B) travelers

   (C) trains

   (D) honors

16. The wild _____ escaped from the net.

   (F) pupil

   (G) driver

   (H) beast

   (J) spider

17. Our field trip to the _____ was interesting.

   (A) backyard

   (B) upstairs

   (C) traffic

   (D) museum

18. The _____ crowed at dawn.

   (F) lion

   (G) giraffe

   (H) rooster

   (J) sparrow

19. We squeezed down a _____ hallway.

   (A) wooden

   (B) narrow

   (C) foolish

   (D) prize

Directions: Read each item. Choose the word that means the same thing as the underlined word.

20. The dinner was <u>excellent</u>.

   (F) very good

   (G) above

   (H) higher

   (J) unpleasant

21. No one could <u>capture</u> the wild tiger.

   (A) range

   (B) hunt

   (C) catch

   (D) release

22. We need his pitching <u>skill</u> on our team.

   (F) toss

   (G) curve

   (H) dance

   (J) talent

STOP

Practice Test 1: Reading
Part 2: Reading Comprehension

Directions: Read the passage, and answer the questions that follow.

The Surprise

Grace had a cocoon in a jar that she kept in the garage. She had found the cocoon on a bush. Grace decided to take her cocoon to school. The class had a white rat, a turtle, and three goldfish. Now, they could have a butterfly, too! Grace knew Ms. Carr would not mind an addition to the class.

"Are you sure that a butterfly will come out of this cocoon, Grace?" asked Ms. Carr when Grace showed her the jar.

"Oh, yes, I'm sure," Grace answered. "And I think it will hatch any day now."

Two days later, Grace was the first student in the classroom. She ran to the jar. Inside was a large, gray insect with a thick, furry body. "What is it?" Grace asked, wrinkling her nose.

Ms. Carr smiled. "It's a moth," she said. "See how its wings are open, even though it's resting? Let's take this moth outside and watch it try its wings!"

1. This story is mostly about

(A) a girl who wants to raise turtles.

(B) a girl who is surprised when a cocoon hatches into a moth.

(C) a teacher who likes moths.

(D) a teacher who is disappointed to see a moth in a jar.

2. This story suggests that

(F) both butterflies and moths hatch from cocoons.

(G) butterflies are difficult to raise.

(H) all children like animals and insects.

(J) teachers should not have animals in classrooms.

3. Which of these statements is a fact from the story?

(A) Ms. Carr is a substitute teacher.

(B) Ms. Carr seems uninterested in her students.

(C) Ms. Carr knows how to tell a moth from a butterfly.

(D) Ms. Carr must not like moths.

GO

Practice Test 1: Reading
Part 2: Reading Comprehension

Directions: Read the selection, and answer the questions that follow.

Birthday Party Blues

My birthday party was supposed to be outside, so of course it was raining. All of my guests were soaking wet. My presents were soaking wet, too. I had planned some games, but my friends were acting strangely. They kept whispering to each other all through the party games.

When it was time to open my presents, it turned out that all seven of my friends had bought me the same gift! How many copies of *Map Zap* software does one person need? It was hard to keep saying thank you and sound grateful each time. My friends seemed to think that the whole thing was really funny. They could not stop snickering.

Then, it was time to open my present from my parents. Mom handed me a gift, and I ripped off the paper. *Map Zap* again! But Mom grinned and said, "Look inside, Darcy." Inside the box was a photograph of a puppy sitting in front of a pile of gifts. Underneath the pictures, it said, "I'm waiting in the garage." I raced outside in the rain to the garage door. There was my new puppy, Snoopy, and the real gifts my friends had brought me. What a great party!

4. What is the main idea of this story?

(F) a birthday party that seems to go badly

(G) a little dog who goes to a birthday party

(H) a joke played on Darcy by her friends

(J) a party take place inside because of rain

5. What is *Map Zap*?

(A) a history book

(B) computer software

(C) a book about maps

(D) a board game

6. Why do you think Darcy's friends were whispering during the games?

(F) because the games were strange

(G) because they were winning all the prizes

(H) because they all were going to play a joke on Darcy

(J) because they like talking

7. Which of the following is an opinion?

(A) Darcy received a puppy as a gift.

(B) Darcy's party was supposed to be outside.

(C) Darcy got eight copies of *Map Zap*.

(D) This had to be Darcy's best birthday ever.

Practice Test 1: Reading
Part 2: Reading Comprehension

Directions: Read the selection, and answer the questions that follow.

Up, Up, and Away

Malik climbed into the basket on that cold morning, and he shivered. When the basket tipped from side to side, he gasped. While Dad was climbing in, the pilot twisted something, and fire shot up into the air. Malik jumped.

"It's all right," said the pilot. "I'm doing this to heat the air in the balloon." Malik tipped back his head. High above him was the opening of the huge, bright balloon. He looked over the edge of the basket. It was tied with ropes to keep it close to the ground. But suddenly, it started to rock and rise up.

"Here we go!" said Dad, smiling happily at Malik.

Malik bit his lip. "I'm not sure I'm going to like this," he said.

People on the ground untied the ropes, and the balloon with its basket of passengers kept rising up into the air. It wasn't like taking off in an airplane. Instead, the balloon was floating up gently into the morning sky.

Soon, Malik, Dad, and the pilot could see far across the trees. "Look, there's the lake!" said Dad. Malik saw a blue patch on the ground. Lake Clooney was suddenly tiny! The trees looked like green cotton balls. The fields looked like pieces of a quilt.

As the balloon floated on, Malik felt less and less afraid. He started pointing at things, too. "Look, Dad! There's my school! And there's our house!" Malik could see his tree house in the backyard and the shed where he kept his bicycle. The whole house and yard looked smaller than one of his thumbnails. Then, Malik looked ahead into the blue sky. The sun was starting to shine. It was the perfect day to fly in a hot-air balloon.

Name _____ Date _____

Practice Test 1: Reading
Part 2: Reading Comprehension

Directions: Answer the questions about the story on page 62.

8. This story is mostly about

(F) a boy who sees his school from the air.

(G) a boy and his father who learn about flight.

(H) a boy and his father who fly in a hot-air balloon.

(J) a boy and his father who learn how to fly.

9. Malik's house and yard look smaller than

(A) the lake.

(B) the balloon.

(C) the trees.

(D) his thumbnail.

10. How can you tell Malik is nervous at first?

(F) He climbs into the basket and looks at the ground.

(G) He gasps, jumps, and bites his lip.

(H) He smiles at his father.

(J) He sees his school and his house.

11. Which of these statements is an opinion?

(A) "I'm doing this to heat the air in the balloon."

(B) "Here we go!"

(C) "I'm not sure I'm going to like this."

(D) "Look, there's the lake!"

12. Choose the word that best describes Dad's feeling about the balloon ride.

(F) worried

(G) quiet

(H) excited

(J) interested

13. Choose another title for this passage.

(A) "My House and Yard"

(B) "Hot-Air Balloon History"

(C) "Malik's Balloon Ride"

(D) "Fast Flying"

GO

Practice Test 1: Reading
Part 2: Reading Comprehension

Directions: Read the selection. Then, answer the questions on the following page.

Johnny Appleseed

There are many tall tales about the life of Johnny Appleseed. But the facts may surprise you!

There was a real Johnny Appleseed. His given name was *John Chapman*. He grew up with his nine brothers and sisters in Longmeadow, Massachusetts. John always loved trees and wild animals. When he was 23 years old, John began walking west, carrying only a gun, hatchet, and knapsack. He walked more than 300 miles. Sometimes he wore shoes, but sometimes he walked barefoot.

As he passed the cider mills in eastern Pennsylvania, John asked if he could have some of the mill's apple seeds. Then, he found a piece of empty land and planted the seeds. He did this several times in Ohio and Indiana, too. When the seeds grew into <u>saplings</u>, John went back to dig up the young trees. Then, he sold them to pioneers who were starting farms. These settlers wanted apples to make apple butter, cider, and vinegar. John gave away saplings for free to people who wanted the trees but were too poor to pay for them.

As John walked from place to place, he brought not only trees, but news, stories, and books. When he stayed with a family, he would read to them and then lend them books.

John lived until the age of 71. When he died, he left behind 15,000 apple trees and more than 2,000 saplings for pioneer families to enjoy.

Practice Test 1: Reading
Part 2: Reading Comprehension

Directions: Answer the questions about the selection on page 64.

14. Another title that shows the main idea of this passage is

(F) "John Chapman, Hiker."

(G) "The Man Who Walked Across America."

(H) "How Apple Trees Went East."

(J) "John Chapman: The Apple-Tree Man."

15. About how many apple trees did John Chapman leave behind?

(A) 300

(B) 2,000

(C) 15,000

(D) 50,000

16. Why do you think that John Chapman grew trees?

(F) because he loved trees and could also earn a living growing them

(G) because he wanted to eat apples all the time

(H) because he wanted to make a lot of money

(J) because he wanted to create more forests

17. Choose a correct fact from the passage.

(A) John Chapman planted trees all over America.

(B) John Chapman brought apple trees to Pennsylvania, Ohio, and Indiana.

(C) John Chapman planted more than 100,000 trees in his lifetime.

(D) John Chapman was not able to read.

18. Which of the following does this story lead you to believe?

(F) John Chapman played a big part in helping pioneer families.

(G) John Chapman probably did not like books very much.

(H) John Chapman died a very rich man.

(J) John Chapman was an unhappy person.

19. What is the meaning of the word *sapling*?

(A) maple syrup

(B) tree sap

(C) a type of seed

(D) a young tree

GO

Practice Test 1: Reading
Part 2: Reading Comprehension
Directions: Read the selection, and answer the questions that follow.

Sign Language

Sign language is used by people who are not able to hear or speak well. They use their hands instead of their voices to talk. Their hand signals may be different letters, words, or whole ideas.

Sign language is used by other people, too. Have you ever watched a football or basketball game? The referees use hand signals to let people know what has happened in the game. Signs can mean *foul*, *time out*, or can let players know when a play was good.

Guess who else uses sign language? You do! You wave your hand for *hello* and *goodbye*. You nod your head up and down to say *yes* and back and forth to say *no*. You point to show which way to go. Sign language is used by people everywhere to communicate.

20. What is the main idea of this passage?

(F) Sign language is used by people who cannot hear well.

(G) Sign language is important to many sports.

(H) Sign language is not used in all countries.

(J) Sign language is used by people everywhere.

21. Which of the following is an example of sign language?

(A) calling out the name of your friend

(B) singing a song

(C) waving *hello* or *goodbye*

(D) talking on the telephone

22. Which of these is another example of sign language?

(F) rocking a baby to sleep

(G) raising your hand in class

(H) running down the sidewalk to school

(J) jumping rope

23. Which of the following is an opinion?

(A) Sign language is a way to communicate.

(B) Sign language is very interesting.

(C) Sign language is used in sports.

(D) Sign language is done with hand signals.

STOP

Name _____ Date _____

Capitalization

Directions: Choose the answer that is missing a capital letter. If no capital letters are missing, choose "None."

Example

- (A) The snow
- (B) started to fall
- (C) in December.
- (D) None

Answer: (D)

1. (A) she went
- (B) to the basement
- (C) to get the laundry.
- (D) None

2. (F) My favorite
- (G) book is
- (H) *charlotte's Web.*
- (J) None

3. (A) My family
- (B) went on a trip
- (C) to ohio.
- (D) None

4. (F) Oliver knows
- (G) he isn't
- (H) supposed to do that.
- (J) None

5. (A) I want
- (B) to read the book
- (C) *The Light in the window.*
- (D) None

6. (F) did you
- (G) find your gift
- (H) on the table?
- (J) None

Remember— sentences and proper nouns start with capital letters.

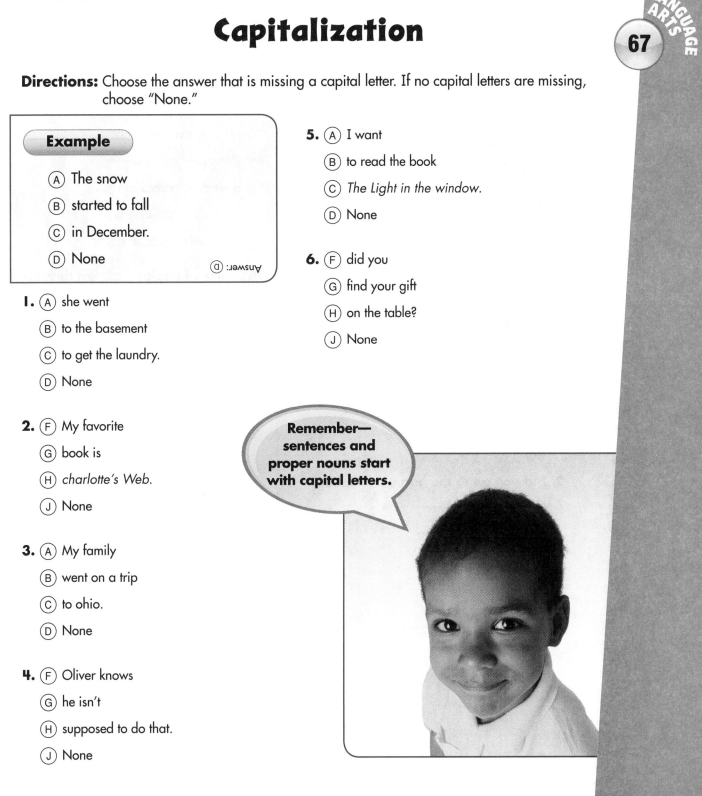

Name _____ Date _____

Capitalization

Directions: Choose the answer that has the correct capitalization.

Example

My last teacher was _____.

(A) ms. Smith

(B) Ms. smith

(C) Ms. Smith

(D) ms. smith

Answer: C

---

1. The bus arrived at _____ more than three hours late.

(A) the Station

(B) The station

(C) The Station

(D) the station

2. Did you go to the game on _____?

(F) saturday afternoon

(G) Saturday afternoon

(H) Saturday Afternoon

(J) saturday Afternoon

3. Angela is my _____.

(A) favorite cousin

(B) Favorite cousin

(C) favorite Cousin

(D) Favorite Cousin

4. Samir's mom works at _____.

(F) Greendale public Library

(G) greendale public library

(H) Greendale Public Library

(J) Greendale public library

5. The ruler of England at that time was _____.

(A) king George I

(B) King George I

(C) king george I

(D) King george I

6. School starts on _____.

(F) Tuesday, august 23

(G) tuesday, august 23

(H) tuesday, August 23

(J) Tuesday, August 23

7 . Do you want to go to _____?

(A) the mall

(B) The Mall

(C) The mall

(D) the Mall

Punctuation

Directions: Choose the answer that shows the correct punctuation mark. If no punctuation marks are missing, choose "None."

Example

How many people were at the party?

- Ⓐ .
- Ⓑ ,
- Ⓒ !
- Ⓓ None

Answer: D

1. Look out

- Ⓐ .
- Ⓑ ,
- Ⓒ !
- Ⓓ None

2. Mr Jefferson was mowing his lawn.

- Ⓕ .
- Ⓖ ?
- Ⓗ !
- Ⓙ None

3. Did you get a good grade in math

- Ⓐ .
- Ⓑ ?
- Ⓒ !
- Ⓓ None

First, check to see if the punctuation is missing at the end of the sentence. Next, look for missing punctuation marks inside the sentence.

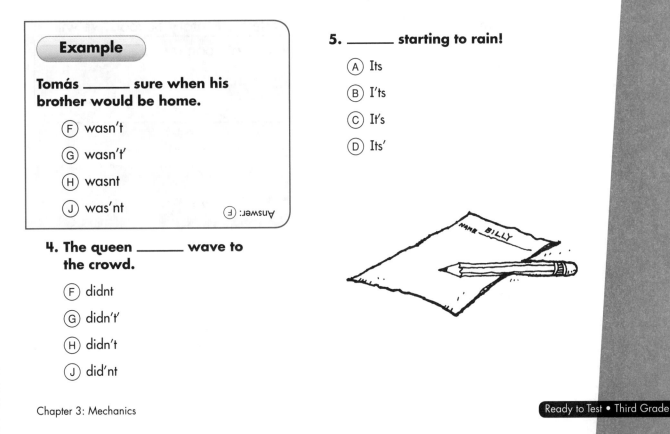

Directions: Choose the answer that shows the correct punctuation.

Example

Tomás _____ sure when his brother would be home.

- Ⓕ wasn't
- Ⓖ wasn't'
- Ⓗ wasnt
- Ⓙ was'nt

Answer: F

4. The queen _____ wave to the crowd.

- Ⓕ didnt
- Ⓖ didn't'
- Ⓗ didn't
- Ⓙ did'nt

5. _____ starting to rain!

- Ⓐ Its
- Ⓑ I'ts
- Ⓒ It's
- Ⓓ Its'

Capitalization and Punctuation

Directions: Choose the answer that shows correct punctuation and capitalization.

Example

Ⓐ Where did you go on your vacation.

Ⓑ We went to california.

Ⓒ Did you like it.

Ⓓ Yes, it was sunny and beautiful.

Answer: Ⓓ

1. Ⓐ What is your favorite city

   Ⓑ I like San francisco.

   Ⓒ It's in California.

   Ⓓ It's where you can find the golden gate Bridge.

2. Ⓕ Nobody answered the door

   Ⓖ knock on the back door.

   Ⓗ Oh, no!

   Ⓙ we woke up mrs. Sobotka.

Directions: Read the letter. Choose the answer that shows the correct capitalization and punctuation for each underlined phrase. Choose "Correct as it is" if the underlined part of the sentence is correct.

October 12 2011
Dear Akiko,
    Please come to the Fall Festival at rowndale Elementary School. We will have games, prizes, and lots of snacks! It starts at noon on Saturday.
Very truly Yours
Ms. Michaels

3. Ⓐ October, 12 2011

   Ⓑ october 12, 2011

   Ⓒ October 12, 2011

   Ⓓ Correct as it is

4. Ⓕ rowndale elementary school

   Ⓖ Rowndale Elementary school

   Ⓗ Rowndale Elementary School

   Ⓙ Correct as it is

5. Ⓐ Very truly yours,

   Ⓑ Very Truly Yours

   Ⓒ Very Truly yours,

   Ⓓ Correct as it is

Spelling

Directions: Choose the word that fits into the sentence and is spelled correctly.

Example

She is not _____ to go.

- (A) eble
- (B) able
- (C) abel
- (D) abell

Answer: (B)

1. Please don't _____ your new shirt.

- (A) winkle
- (B) wrinkle
- (C) wrinkel
- (D) rinkle

2. The _____ is surrounded by flowers.

- (F) fountin
- (G) fontain
- (H) fountein
- (J) fountain

3. Jane treated her book _____.

- (A) carlessly
- (B) carelessly
- (C) carelesly
- (D) carelissly

> Don't forget—you will be looking for both correctly and incorrectly spelled words!

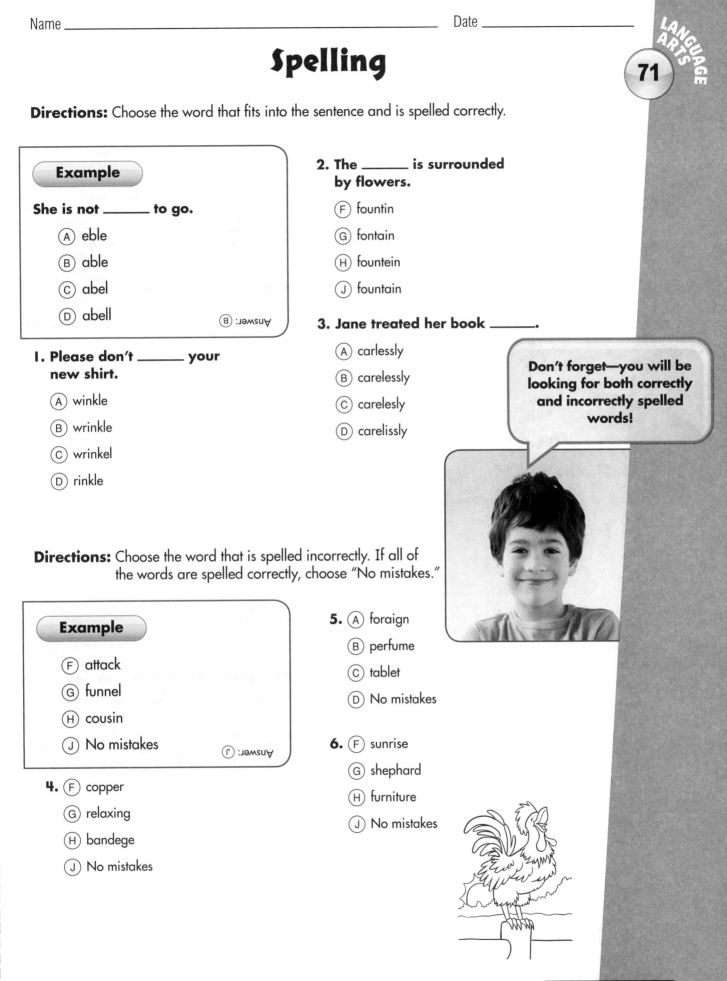

Directions: Choose the word that is spelled incorrectly. If all of the words are spelled correctly, choose "No mistakes."

Example

- (F) attack
- (G) funnel
- (H) cousin
- (J) No mistakes

Answer: (J)

4.
- (F) copper
- (G) relaxing
- (H) bandege
- (J) No mistakes

5.
- (A) foraign
- (B) perfume
- (C) tablet
- (D) No mistakes

6.
- (F) sunrise
- (G) shephard
- (H) furniture
- (J) No mistakes

Name _____ Date _____

Spelling

Directions: Choose the word that is spelled incorrectly.

1. (A) enjineer
   (B) dryer
   (C) mineral
   (D) daisy

2. (F) diary
   (G) nationel
   (H) pronoun
   (J) barrel

3. (A) period
   (B) unusal
   (C) president
   (D) promise

4. (F) curtain
   (G) cryed
   (H) morning
   (J) bath

5. (A) giant
   (B) interesting
   (C) trash
   (D) thousend

6. (F) biology
   (G) vacation
   (H) exemple
   (J) absent

7. (A) agree
   (B) elbow
   (C) wooden
   (D) woolan

8. (F) lonely
   (G) fansy
   (H) ferry
   (J) bacon

Directions: Read each sentence. Look for the underlined word that is spelled incorrectly, and choose that phrase. Choose "No mistakes" if the sentence is correct.

9. (A) My favorite <u>samwich</u>
   (B) is <u>peanut</u> butter
   (C) and grape <u>jelly</u>.
   (D) No mistakes

10. (F) Ella's <u>dollhouse</u>
    (G) has real <u>lites</u>
    (H) and a <u>staircase</u>.
    (J) No mistakes

11. (A) <u>Wolf</u> pups
    (B) play <u>outdoors</u>
    (C) when they are <u>three</u> weeks old.
    (D) No mistakes

12. (F) <u>Thick</u> black smoke
    (G) <u>poored</u> out
    (H) of all the <u>windows</u>.
    (J) No mistakes

Spelling

Directions: Find the underlined word that is not spelled correctly. If all the words are spelled correctly, choose "No mistakes."

1. (A) <u>identify</u> a bird

   (B) bottle of <u>juice</u>

   (C) <u>quiet</u> room

   (D) No mistakes

2. (F) easy <u>lesson</u>

   (G) bright <u>lites</u>

   (H) <u>paddle</u> a canoe

   (J) No mistakes

3. (A) good <u>balance</u>

   (B) <u>runing</u> shoes

   (C) <u>private</u> property

   (D) No mistakes

4. (F) great <u>relief</u>

   (G) our <u>house</u>

   (H) <u>sunnie</u> day

   (J) No mistakes

5. (A) <u>forty</u> years

   (B) <u>twelve</u> pears

   (C) a <u>thousend</u> questions

   (D) No mistakes

Directions: Find the word that is spelled correctly and best completes the sentence.

6. We picked _____ in our garden.

   (F) berries

   (G) berrys

   (H) berrese

   (J) berreis

7. The _____ helped me.

   (A) nourse

   (B) nurce

   (C) nirse

   (D) nurse

8. The answer to this problem is a _____.

   (F) frackshun

   (G) fracteon

   (H) fraction

   (J) fracton

9. Did you _____ the page?

   (A) tare

   (B) tair

   (C) tear

   (D) taer

Sample Test 3: Language Mechanics

Directions: Choose the answer that shows the correct punctuation and capitalization.

1. (A) The bus comes for us at 7:30
   (B) avery likes to ride up front.
   (C) My friends and I like to sit in the back.
   (D) We talk about sports and TV shows?

2. (F) On saturday mornings, we sleep in.
   (G) dad makes pancakes.
   (H) Then, we all work on our chores.
   (J) At the end of the day, We rent a movie to watch.

3. (A) Yesterday, i got a new kitten!
   (B) I named her tara.
   (C) She came from the animal shelter
   (D) She has green eyes and black fur.

4. (F) the house was dark and still.
   (G) Suddenly, the door creaked open!
   (H) Someone inside the house laughed
   (J) It was my friend, sydney, playing a trick!

Directions: Read the passage. Choose the answer that shows the correct capitalization and punctuation for the underlined phrase. Choose "Correct as it is" if the underlined part of the sentence is correct.

lena lopez is my best friend. She gave me a great birthday gift. She got both of us tickets to Bigtop amusement Park. We decided to go on Saturday, May 15, after our gymnastics class. We didn't want to go on the rides first, so we played some games. I won a teddy bear. Then, we ate some hot pretzels. We saved the roller coaster for last!

5. (A) Lena lopez is my Best Friend.
   (B) Lena Lopez is my best friend.
   (C) Lena Lopez is my Best friend.
   (D) Correct as it is

6. (F) Bigtop amusement park
   (G) bigtop amusement park
   (H) Bigtop Amusement Park
   (J) Correct as it is

7. (A) Saturday May 15,
   (B) saturday, May 15
   (C) Saturday, may, 15
   (D) Correct as it is

Sample Test 3: Language Mechanics

Directions: Choose the word that is spelled incorrectly. If all of the words are spelled correctly, choose "No mistakes."

8. (F) writer
(G) cofee
(H) score
(J) No mistakes

9. (A) wrist
(B) resess
(C) lazy
(D) No mistakes

10. (F) finger
(G) addition
(H) supar
(J) No mistakes

11. (A) dangerous
(B) passenger
(C) nature
(D) No mistakes

12. (F) finch
(G) puzzle
(H) vegatable
(J) No mistakes

13. (A) pickel
(B) knick
(C) witch
(D) No mistakes

Directions: Read each choice. Look for the underlined word that is spelled incorrectly. Choose "No mistakes" if the entire sentence is correct.

14. (F) The stilt bird
(G) has thin, red legs
(H) and black faethers.
(J) No mistakes

15. (A) The fir on a rabbit's feet
(B) gives the rabbit
(C) the ability to hop on the snow.
(D) No mistakes

16. (F) Some farmers
(G) raize worms
(H) as a crop.
(J) No mistakes

17. (A) You can bake apples,
(B) make applesauce,
(C) or create delicious pies.
(D) No mistakes

18. (F) Traffick signs
(G) that are colored yellow
(H) warn of changes ahead.
(J) No mistakes

19. (A) Ancient drawings
(B) show the Romans and Greeks
(C) buying candy at shops.
(D) No mistakes

STOP

Nouns and Pronouns

Directions: Read each item. Choose the answer that best completes the sentence.

Example

_____ love to dance.

- Ⓐ He
- Ⓑ She
- Ⓒ They
- Ⓓ Them

Answer: C

1. Dante and Janna gave _____ report today.

- Ⓐ him
- Ⓑ she
- Ⓒ them
- Ⓓ their

2. Please tell _____ to take this note home.

- Ⓕ she
- Ⓖ he
- Ⓗ her
- Ⓙ it

3. _____ called my father on Sunday.

- Ⓐ Him
- Ⓑ He
- Ⓒ Us
- Ⓓ Them

Directions: Choose the answer that could replace the underlined word or words.

Example

Nico built a model rocket.

- Ⓕ Him
- Ⓖ He
- Ⓗ Them
- Ⓙ We

Answer: G

4. Jackson and Leo washed the dishes.

- Ⓕ Him
- Ⓖ Them
- Ⓗ They
- Ⓙ She

5. Did Amanda get her computer repaired?

- Ⓐ her
- Ⓑ she
- Ⓒ it
- Ⓓ us

6. When did you notice the book was missing?

- Ⓕ him
- Ⓖ her
- Ⓗ we
- Ⓙ it

Nouns and Pronouns

Directions: Read each item. Choose the answer that has a mistake.

Example

Ⓐ Do you think them will go shopping?

Ⓑ He doesn't like to eat red meat.

Ⓒ His father is going with him.

Ⓓ They will be back soon.

Answer: Ⓐ

---

1. Ⓐ The dog followed him home.

Ⓑ Him asked if he could keep it.

Ⓒ His parents said that they needed to look for the owner first.

Ⓓ He could keep the dog if the owner couldn't be found.

2. Ⓕ They rode through the mud puddles.

Ⓖ Ahmad and Chloe were laughing, and they couldn't stop.

Ⓗ He was covered with mud.

Ⓙ They bikes were muddy, too.

3. Ⓐ On Saturday, she worked on her hobby.

Ⓑ Her hobby is photography.

Ⓒ Her has taken some good pictures.

Ⓓ We framed one and put it in our family room.

Directions: Choose the answer in which the simple subject is underlined.

4. Ⓕ My father's next book is being printed.

Ⓖ It is about space travel.

Ⓗ My best friend can't wait to read it.

Ⓙ Dad's first book was a big success.

5. Ⓐ We aren't ready to leave yet!

Ⓑ My cousin Sally needs to find her umbrella.

Ⓒ My uncle has lost the map!

Ⓓ This trip is a disaster.

6. Ⓕ You will need yarn, scissors, and paste.

Ⓖ This project is not difficult.

Ⓗ Last spring, my family made one for our table.

Ⓙ The colorful basket turned out well.

Remember, a simple subject does not include adjectives or any other part of speech. Keep it simple!

Verbs

Directions: Read each item. Choose the answer that best completes the sentence.

Example

The gift _____ yesterday.

- (A) arrives
- (B) arrived
- (C) arriving
- (D) will arrive

Answer: (B)

1. Eli and Gina _____ us make bread.

- (A) had help
- (B) will help
- (C) helps
- (D) helping

2. Please _____ this letter to the post office.

- (F) took
- (G) has taken
- (H) tooked
- (J) take

3. No one _____ him about the change of plans.

- (A) telled
- (B) tells
- (C) told
- (D) did tell

4. I _____ a collage for each of my grandparents.

- (F) had maked
- (G) makes
- (H) maked
- (J) made

5. The baby gate _____ after my brother climbed on it.

- (A) broke
- (B) breaked
- (C) breaks
- (D) break

6. The branch must have _____ during the storm last night.

- (F) falls
- (G) fell
- (H) fall
- (J) fallen

Not sure which answer is correct?

Try reading each choice softly out loud to yourself. Shhhh!

Verbs

Directions: Choose the answer that uses an incorrect verb.

Example

(A) The library have a room for music.

(B) In the room, you can listen to CDs.

(C) It also has lots of books about music.

(D) I love spending time there.

Answer: (A)

---

1. (A) I like to collect seashells.

(B) I has more than 60 types in my collection.

(C) I find most of them on trips to the beach.

(D) My cousins send me some from their trips, too.

2. (F) On cold days, Mom makes soup.

(G) I help to chop the vegetables.

(H) The soup simmer all afternoon.

(J) It makes our whole house smell cozy.

3. (A) Darius chewed on a nail nervously.

(B) When the ball hit the bat, he begun to run.

(C) He rounded the bases as fast as he could.

(D) Darius grinned as he slid into home.

4. (F) Li pick up her heavy backpack.

(G) She carries that backpack everywhere.

(H) It has all her art supplies in it.

(J) She also carries her laptop in the backpack.

5. (A) He forgot to take his jacket home.

(B) It were a cold day.

(C) He shivered without his jacket.

(D) He was very glad to get home at last.

6. (F) Nobody is home today.

(G) The house is locked up.

(H) It look strange with the shades down.

(J) I am not used to seeing it so empty.

Does a question seem too tricky?

Just skip it, and come back to it later.

Name _____   Date _____

Adjectives

80

Directions: Read each item. Choose the answer that best completes the sentence.

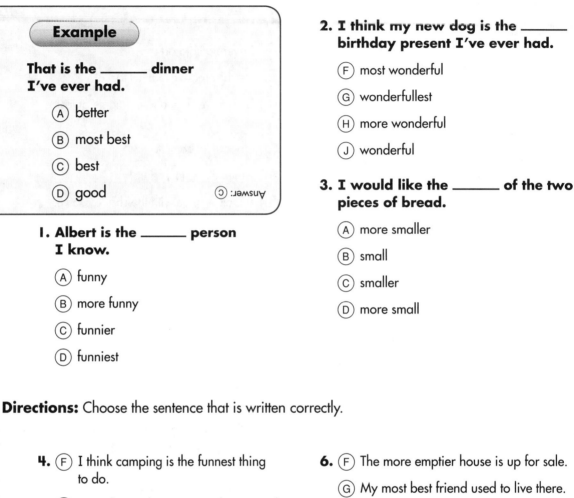

Example

That is the _____ dinner
I've ever had.

(A) better

(B) most best

(C) best

(D) good

Answer: C

1. Albert is the _____ person
I know.

(A) funny

(B) more funny

(C) funnier

(D) funniest

2. I think my new dog is the _____
birthday present I've ever had.

(F) most wonderful

(G) wonderfullest

(H) more wonderful

(J) wonderful

3. I would like the _____ of the two
pieces of bread.

(A) more smaller

(B) small

(C) smaller

(D) more small

Directions: Choose the sentence that is written correctly.

4. (F) I think camping is the funnest thing
to do.

(G) We take our biggest tent, the one with
the little window.

(H) We find the more quiet campsite
we can.

(J) Our favoriter place is by a little lake in
the woods.

5. (A) This is my most better coat.

(B) It is the brightest red that I've ever seen.

(C) It is also more warmer than
my other coats.

(D) This more good coat is my favorite.

6. (F) The more emptier house is up for sale.

(G) My most best friend used to live there.

(H) Her mother is the kindest person I know.

(J) I was so saddest to see them
move away.

Adjectives

Directions: Read each item. Choose the sentence in which an adjective is underlined.

Example

(A) The school bake sale <u>starts</u> at 8:00.

(B) Everyone has made <u>delicious</u> treats.

(C) I love Mrs. Petrus's blueberry <u>muffins</u>.

(D) We brought the <u>leftover</u> items to the food bank.

Answer: (B)

---

1. (A) The new library is in a <u>brick</u> building.

   (B) Clara and Noah looked <u>for</u> books about vegetable gardening.

   (C) The <u>librarian</u> wore a bright red blouse.

   (D) Noah <u>owed</u> four dollars in overdue fines.

2. (F) Two finches have made their <u>nests</u> in our ferns.

   (G) The eggs they laid are <u>pale</u> blue.

   (H) My bird book says the eggs will <u>hatch</u> in about 14 days.

   (J) <u>I</u> can't wait to see the newborn birds!

3. (A) Fiona makes a <u>blanket</u> for her baby sister.

   (B) <u>She</u> cuts out squares of soft fabrics.

   (C) Mom <u>helps</u> her pin them together in a pretty pattern.

   (D) Fiona hopes this will be the baby's <u>favorite</u> blanket.

4. (F) The <u>sky</u> grew darker and darker.

   (G) Thunder rumbled, and lightning <u>streaked</u> the sky.

   (H) Suddenly, <u>large</u> drops of rain pelted the roof.

   (J) In the distance, sirens <u>began</u> to wail.

5. (A) The <u>firefighter</u> pointed the hose at the truck.

   (B) She <u>loved</u> seeing the dirt and grime wash away.

   (C) The bright <u>red</u> truck shone in the sun.

   (D) Engine 6 was ready for the next <u>call</u>!

6. (F) The <u>crowd</u> went wild.

   (G) Justin <u>hit</u> a home run.

   (H) My small school won the <u>championship</u>.

   (J) We even got a <u>shiny</u> trophy.

Sample Test 4: Grammar

Directions: Choose the answer that best completes the sentence.

1. Rico asked _____ coach for advice.

   (A) him

   (B) his

   (C) them

   (D) her

2. Will _____ sisters meet us after the movie?

   (F) she

   (G) he

   (H) her

   (J) it

3. _____ are leaving for Chicago next Sunday.

   (A) Him

   (B) Us

   (C) Them

   (D) They

Directions: Choose the answer that could replace the underlined word or words.

4. **Mr. Washington** has never been late for class.

   (F) He

   (G) Him

   (H) It

   (J) Us

5. The baby pointed to **the ambulance** as it drove by.

   (A) her

   (B) him

   (C) we

   (D) it

6. **Sonya and Connor** tied for first place.

   (F) Him

   (G) Them

   (H) She

   (J) They

GO

Name _____ Date _____

Sample Test 4: Grammar

Directions: Read each item. Choose the answer that best completes the sentence.

7. **Mr. Bentley _____ us with the math lesson.**

   Ⓐ don't help

   Ⓑ will help

   Ⓒ would helping

   Ⓓ helping

8. **Please _____ the band uniform tomorrow.**

   Ⓕ buy

   Ⓖ buyed

   Ⓗ bought

   Ⓙ boughten

9. **Kara _____ us about her trip to Scotland yesterday.**

   Ⓐ telled

   Ⓑ told

   Ⓒ tells

   Ⓓ did told

10. **Jada _____ to hike with her family.**

   Ⓕ did liked

   Ⓖ liking

   Ⓗ likes

   Ⓙ like

Directions: Read each item. Choose the word or phrase that best completes the sentence.

11. **Drew is the _____ person I have met.**

   Ⓐ sincere

   Ⓑ sincerer

   Ⓒ more sincere

   Ⓓ most sincere

12. **The _____ puppy will get tired before the other puppies.**

   Ⓕ most energetic

   Ⓖ energetic

   Ⓗ energeticer

   Ⓙ energeticest

13. **Please give me the _____ doll on the shelf.**

   Ⓐ largest

   Ⓑ more large

   Ⓒ most large

   Ⓓ larger

STOP

Subject-Verb Agreement

Directions: Choose the answer that best completes the sentence.

Example

Ebony and Brianna _____ Bo for a walk every day.

- Ⓐ takes
- Ⓑ take
- Ⓒ taked
- Ⓓ will takes

Answer: (B)

1. Chan and Audrey _____ their kites together.

- Ⓐ make
- Ⓑ makes
- Ⓒ has made
- Ⓓ maked

2. _____ her parents coming to the concert?

- Ⓕ Is
- Ⓖ Are
- Ⓗ Am
- Ⓙ Was

3. _____ spoke to my mother on Parents' Night.

- Ⓐ Him
- Ⓑ He
- Ⓒ Us
- Ⓓ Them

4. Antonio _____ to his guitar lesson on Thursdays.

- Ⓕ has went
- Ⓖ go
- Ⓗ gone
- Ⓙ goes

5. The small tree _____ its leaves first every autumn.

- Ⓐ loosed
- Ⓑ lose
- Ⓒ loses
- Ⓓ losts

6. Sanj and Maya _____ planning to go to the concert.

- Ⓕ is
- Ⓖ are
- Ⓗ am
- Ⓙ was

7. Darius and Logan _____ to the beach yesterday.

- Ⓐ goes
- Ⓑ had went
- Ⓒ went
- Ⓓ has gone

Subject-Verb Agreement

Directions: Choose the answer that uses an incorrect verb.

1. (A) The skipper steer the boat.

   (B) The wind blew across the lake.

   (C) The boat stayed on course.

   (D) The brave skipper brought the boat safely to shore.

2. (F) The dentist cleaned my teeth.

   (G) I was worried he might have to use the drill.

   (H) He were very nice.

   (J) My teeth are shiny now!

3. (A) The pioneer chose his land carefully.

   (B) He wanted a stream near his cabin.

   (C) He want good land for crops.

   (D) He knew he could use the trees for building.

4. (F) Abigail Adams was born in 1744.

   (G) Women were not given much schooling in those days.

   (H) Abigail were allowed to study and read as much as she wanted to.

   (J) Abigail and John Adams got married in 1764.

5. (A) Paper is made from tree logs.

   (B) Logs is shipped to paper mills.

   (C) The bark is removed from the logs.

   (D) Next, they are cut into thin chips.

6. (F) Ari broke his leg last week.

   (G) His parents brought him a bunch of books from the library.

   (H) They wanted to keep him busy!

   (J) Callie and Zane signs his cast.

7. (A) Sierra went fishing with her grandpa.

   (B) She put a worm on the hook.

   (C) They both throws out their lines.

   (D) She caught a bigger fish than him!

Name _____   Date _____

Sentences

Directions: Read each item. Choose the sentence that is written correctly.

Example

  (A) Mr. Woo opens his store early.

  (B) Always kind to us.

  (C) Food and other things.

  (D) Like to shop there.

Answer: (A)

1. (A) We are going on a trip.

  (B) To Japan, China, and Korea.

  (C) Packing our suitcases.

  (D) Can't wait to travel and have fun!

2. (F) Jars of paint out.

  (G) Painting of trees and flowers.

  (H) I am going to paint for an hour.

  (J) Wonderful to have art class.

3. (A) The American flag.

  (B) Red, white, and blue.

  (C) Thirteen stripes, one for each colony.

  (D) Our flag today has 50 stars.

4. (F) Caleb finished lunch at one o'clock.

  (G) Chicken sandwich, juice, and an apple.

  (H) All packed in a brown paper bag.

  (J) Caleb's lunch hour over.

5. (A) The train is coming down the tracks.

  (B) Can hear the rumbling of the train.

  (C) A bright headlight and a loud whistle.

  (D) Fifty cars and a caboose.

> **Give each answer choice the true-false test. This can help you narrow down your choices.**

Sentences

Directions: Read each item. Choose the sentence that is written incorrectly.

1. (A) Darby stood at the window.

   (B) He watched quietly for a minute.

   (C) Then, his ears stood up.

   (D) Jumping and barking wildly.

2. (F) A tree is a system.

   (G) Parts that work together are called a *system*.

   (H) A tree has roots, a trunk, limbs, and leaves.

   (J) Work together to help the tree grow.

3. (A) Tia and her grandpa went to the bookstore.

   (B) Tia needed a new dictionary.

   (C) Had a lot of pictures.

   (D) She wanted one that was more grown-up.

4. (F) Weathering wears down rocks.

   (G) Wind, water, ice, and chemicals.

   (H) It changes the shapes or forms of rocks.

   (J) Soil is made of weathered rocks.

5. (A) Rosie's parents speak Chinese.

   (B) Want Rosie to learn it, too.

   (C) They speak Chinese on the weekends.

   (D) Someday, they will all visit China together.

6. (F) Joni needs a new coat.

   (G) She likes the pink one.

   (H) Too much money.

   (J) She picks out the blue one instead.

7. (A) Jon and Joey like soccer.

   (B) Joey also likes baseball.

   (C) Jon do not like baseball.

   (D) They are best friends.

8. (F) Amy sees a butterfly.

   (G) Beautiful summer day.

   (H) Shes watches it fly.

   (J) It is yellow and blue.

Sentences

Directions: Choose the best combination of the underlined sentences.

Example

It rained like cats and dogs.
It rained all night long.

Ⓐ Like cats and dogs, it rained all night long.

Ⓑ It rained all night long, and like cats and dogs.

Ⓒ It rained like cats and dogs, and it rained all night long.

Ⓓ It rained like cats and dogs all night long.

Answer: Ⓓ

1. I like pizza for dinner.
I like mushroom pizza.

Ⓐ I like mushroom pizza, and I like it for dinner.

Ⓑ I like pizza, mushroom pizza, for dinner.

Ⓒ I like mushroom pizza for dinner.

Ⓓ I like pizza for dinner, and I like mushroom pizza.

2. Parrots live in the tropics.
Parrots are beautiful birds.

Ⓕ Parrots are beautiful birds that live in the tropics.

Ⓖ Parrots, beautiful birds, live in the tropics.

Ⓗ Parrots live in the tropics and are beautiful birds.

Ⓙ Parrots, that live in the tropics, are beautiful birds.

3. The trees are in the forest.
The trees are tall.

Ⓐ The trees are in the forest, and are tall.

Ⓑ The tall trees, they are in the forest.

Ⓒ The trees in the forest are tall.

Ⓓ The trees, tall, are in the forest.

4. The birds come to the feeder.
The birds are red and blue.

Ⓕ The red and blue birds come to the feeder.

Ⓖ The birds, red and blue, come to the feeder.

Ⓗ The birds are red and blue, and they come to the feeder.

Ⓙ The birds come to the feeder, red and blue.

5. Field Day is my favorite day at school.
Field Day is May 10.

Ⓐ Field Day is my favorite day at school, and it is May 10.

Ⓑ Field Day, my favorite day at school, is May 10.

Ⓒ Field Day is May 10, my favorite day at school.

Ⓓ Field Day is my favorite day, May 10, at school.

Sentences

Directions: Read the letter. For each item, decide which version of the sentence is correct. If the sentence needs no changes, choose "Correct as it is."

Dear Ms. Wood,

(1) Our whole class would like to thank you for the nature trail tour. (2) We was amazed at the number of flowers, and animals, on the trail. (3) The birds and animals, all of them that we saw, were so beautiful. (4) We drew pictures of some of the birds and animals after we got back to school. (5) The wildflowers, which we saw on the nature trail, were colorful and interesting. (6) Our favorite was the one called *Queen Anne's lace.* (7) We are sending you a drawing of this flower as a thank-you for the tour.

Sincerely,
Mrs. Coletti's Third-Grade Class

1. Sentence 2 is best written

(A) We were amazed by the number of flowers, and animals, on the trail.

(B) The flowers and animals was amazing on the trail.

(C) We were amazed at the number of flowers and animals on the trail.

(D) Correct as it is

2. Sentence 3 is best written

(F) The birds and animals that we seen were so beautiful.

(G) All of the birds and animals we saw were so beautiful.

(H) All of the birds and all of the animals we saw were so beautiful.

(J) Correct as it is

3. Sentence 5 is best written

(A) The wildflowers that we saw on the nature trail were colorful and interesting.

(B) We saw on the trail wildflowers which were colorful and interesting.

(C) Wildflowers, colorful and interesting, which we saw on the trail.

(D) Correct as it is

4. Sentence 7 is best written

(F) We are sending you this flower, a drawing, as a thank-you for the tour.

(G) As a thank-you, we are sending you this drawing, of this flower.

(H) Thank-you for the tour, we are sending you this drawing of a flower.

(J) Correct as it is

Paragraphs

Directions: Read each paragraph. Then, choose the best topic sentence for the paragraph.

Example

_____ After President John Adams moved in, the outside was painted white. However, the name *White House* did not come into use until much later, when President Theodore Roosevelt had the name put on his writing paper.

Ⓐ The president's house was not always known as the *White House.*

Ⓑ George Washington did not want to live in the White House.

Ⓒ The White House was burned down during the War of 1812.

Ⓓ President Roosevelt, who lived in the White House, loved to ride horses.

Answer: Ⓐ

1. _____ Some sand looks white and seems to sparkle. Sand can also be light tan, black, or even pink. Sand is the same color as the rocks from which it was made. Looking at sand under a magnifying glass makes it possible to see the sparkling colors more clearly.

Ⓐ Sand can be made of large or small grains.

Ⓑ All sand looks about the same.

Ⓒ Not all sand looks the same.

Ⓓ The color of sand is very important.

2. _____ They help keep bits of dust from getting in our eyes. They act as umbrellas, keeping the rain from our eyes. They also help shade our eyes from the sun. Like the frame around a beautiful painting, eyelashes play an important part in keeping our eyes safe.

Ⓕ Eyelashes can be blonde, brown, or black.

Ⓖ Eyelashes protect our eyes from harm.

Ⓗ Do you have long eyelashes?

Ⓙ Eyelashes can be straight or curly.

Remember, a paragraph should contain one main idea. All of the sentences should be about that idea.

Chapter 5: Usage

Paragraphs

Directions: Read the topic sentence. Choose the answer that best develops the topic sentence.

1. The canary is one of the most well-liked pet birds.

(A) Canaries are not only pretty, but they sing cheerful songs.

(B) Canaries can be red, yellow, or orange.

(C) You have to be careful with a pet bird, or it may escape.

(D) Canaries like to live in the Canary Islands.

2. Some animals and insects are speedy creatures.

(F) Hummingbirds and dragonflies can fly at speeds of more than 30 miles per hour.

(G) Snails move very slowly.

(H) Ducks and hummingbirds are both birds.

(J) There are animals that are fast and some that are slow.

Directions: Read the paragraph, and answer the questions that follow.

(1) These people face some difficulties in looking at the world around them. (2) To the color blind, for example, red and green look like the same colors. (3) A color-blind person may have trouble telling a ripe tomato from an unripe one. (4) There are also some people who cannot see any colors. (5) To them, everything looks black, white, or gray.

3. Choose the best topic sentence for this paragraph.

(A) People who cannot tell one color from another are said to be color blind.

(B) To these people, the world looks mostly yellow and brown.

(C) A color-blind person cannot see any colors.

(D) Red and green are hard to tell apart.

4. Choose the best last sentence for this paragraph.

(F) Color blindness can make some tasks difficult.

(G) Color blindness creates special challenges but does not keep people from leading normal lives.

(H) People with color blindness look like other people.

(J) Some animals are color blind, too.

Paragraphs

Directions: Read the selection, and answer the questions that follow.

(1) Measure out about four spoonfuls of water and one spoonful of sugar in a very small, open bottle. (2) Paint the bottle red. (3) Then, hang the bottle under an overhanging roof or near a window. (4) If you plant red flowers, they will help, too. (5) The tiny hummingbirds will come to drink the sugar water. (6) The hummingbird will think that the bright feeder is another flower and the sugar water is flower nectar. (7) Hummingbirds like brightly-colored flowers that have lots of nectar.

1. Choose the best topic sentence for this paragraph.

(A) Here's how to attract hummingbirds to your backyard.

(B) Hummingbirds are among the fastest flyers in the bird world.

(C) Do you like hummingbirds?

(D) Hummingbirds are colorful birds.

2. Choose a sentence to take out of the selection.

(F) Sentence 1

(G) Sentence 3

(H) Sentence 4

(J) Sentence 6

3. Choose a better place for Sentence 7.

(A) between Sentence 1 and Sentence 2

(B) between Sentence 2 and Sentence 3

(C) between Sentence 3 and Sentence 4

(D) between Sentence 5 and Sentence 6

4. Choose the best sentence to add to the end of the selection.

(F) Hummingbirds are as brightly colored as the flowers they like best.

(G) Hummingbirds are fast flyers and dart from place to place.

(H) By building a simple feeder, you can help hummingbirds and enjoy them in your yard.

(J) By building a simple feeder, you can trick hummingbirds.

Study Skills

Directions: Read each item, and choose the best answer.

Example

Which word comes first in the dictionary?

(A) wood

(B) wool

(C) wander

(D) wand

Answer: D

---

1. Which word comes first in the dictionary?

(A) reef

(B) relief

(C) real

(D) repeat

2. Which word comes first in the dictionary?

(F) narrow

(G) native

(H) none

(J) noon

If two answer choices look a lot alike, one of them is probably correct.

3. Which word comes first in the dictionary?

(A) bless

(B) belt

(C) bear

(D) blue

4. Which word comes first in the dictionary?

(F) ditch

(G) dine

(H) din

(J) dial

5. Look at the guide words. Which word would be found on the page?

clean	cliff

(A) clock

(B) climate

(C) clog

(D) clear

6. Look at the guide words. Which word would be found on the page?

empty	enemy

(F) empire

(G) enchant

(H) engrave

(J) enter

Study Skills

Directions: Use the table of contents and index to answer the questions.

Remember, a **table of contents** gives you the names of chapters or topics. An **index** shows you where specific information is found.

1. In which chapter would you look for information about butterflies?

(A) Chapter 3

(B) Chapter 4

(C) Chapter 5

(D) Chapter 6

2. There is some information about mice on page _____.

(F) 15

(G) 105

(H) 90

(J) 55

3. To find out about rainforest animals, turn to pages _____.

(A) 60–64

(B) 103–107

(C) 39–41

(D) 14–15

4. Which chapter would you read to learn about rats?

(F) Chapter 1

(G) Chapter 2

(H) Chapter 3

(J) Chapter 4

5. If you wanted information on blue whales, you would turn to page _____.

(A) 60

(B) 61

(C) 62

(D) 64

6. Where would you look to find information about the Seattle Zoo?

(F) Chapter 1

(G) Chapter 2

(H) Chapter 3

(J) Chapter 4

Study Skills

Directions: Read each question, and choose the best answer.

1. Where would you look to find information about today's weather?

Ⓐ online

Ⓑ in a history book

Ⓒ in a dictionary

Ⓓ in an encyclopedia

2. Where would you look to check the spelling of *emergency*?

Ⓕ in a newspaper

Ⓖ in a history book

Ⓗ in a dictionary

Ⓙ in an encyclopedia

3. Where would you look to find out who was the twelfth president?

Ⓐ in a newspaper

Ⓑ in an atlas

Ⓒ in a dictionary

Ⓓ in an encyclopedia

Directions: Use the dictionary entries below to answer the following questions.

save [sāv] *v.* 1. to rescue from harm or danger 2. to keep in a safe condition 3. to set aside for future use; store
saving [sā´vǐng] *n.* 1. rescuing from harm or danger 2. avoiding excess spending; economy 3. something saved
savory [sā´və-rē] *adj.* 1. appealing to the taste or smell 2. salty to the taste; not sweet

4. Which sentence uses *savory* the same way it is used in definition 2?

Ⓕ After I ate the savory stew, I was thirsty.

Ⓖ The savory bank opened an account for me.

Ⓗ This flower has a savory scent.

Ⓙ The savory dog rescued me from harm.

5. The *a* in *saving* sounds most like the *a* in _____.

Ⓐ pat

Ⓑ ape

Ⓒ heated

Ⓓ naughty

Study Skills

Directions: Decide where the information in each item is most likely to be found. Write the letter of your answer on the line.

> **A.** in an atlas
> **B.** in a dictionary
> **C.** in an encyclopedia
> **D.** in a newspaper

1. _____ pronunciation of a word

2. _____ types of animals in a rainforest

3. _____ map of Pennsylvania

4. _____ comic strip

5. _____ place where Abraham Lincoln was born

6. _____ report of a fire in your neighborhood

7. _____ definition of the word *concave*

8. _____ latitude and longitude of Paris, France

9. _____ local job listings

10. _____ the date that World War II ended

11. _____ how to break a word into syllables

Directions: Choose the best answer to each question.

12. *What I remember most about that big, old house in Iowa was the kitchen, a room that was warm and always smelled wonderful.*

    This sentence would most likely be found in _____.

    (A) a newspaper article

    (B) an autobiography

    (C) an encyclopedia

    (D) a science book

13. **Which of these sentences would most likely be found in a newspaper article?**

    (F) "Now hold on there," said the sheriff. "We don't put up with things like that in this town."

    (G) It wasn't a star they were looking at, but a spaceship, and it was coming right at them.

    (H) Guido said goodbye to his family, picked up his bags, and joined the crowd walking toward the ship.

    (J) A recent report from the school board stated that there are more students in our school than there were last year.

Sample Test 5: Usage

Directions: Read the journal entry. For each item, decide which version of the sentence is correct. If the sentence needs no changes, choose "Correct as it is."

(1) My parents and I, we are flying to Chicago tomorrow. (2) My mom is attending a business conference. (3) While Mom is working, Dad and I am seeing the sights. (4) Go to the top of the Hancock Building and the Willis Tower. (5) We will visiting my Aunt Ruth, too. (6) I can hardly wait to go! (7) We are leaving at seven o'clock tomorrow morning.

1. Sentence 1 is best written

- (A) My parents and I are flying to Chicago tomorrow.
- (B) My parents and I were flying to Chicago tomorrow.
- (C) My parents and I, we flew to Chicago tomorrow.
- (D) Correct as it is

2. Sentence 2 is best written

- (F) My mom is attended a business conference.
- (G) My mom will attending a business conference.
- (H) My mom attends a business conference.
- (J) Correct as it is

3. Sentence 3 is best written

- (A) While Mom working, Dad and I will see the sights.
- (B) While Mom is working, Dad and I will see the sights.
- (C) While Mom is working, Dad and I are seen the sights.
- (D) Correct as it is

4. Sentence 5 is best written

- (F) We have visited my Aunt Ruth, too.
- (G) We will be visiting my Aunt Ruth, too.
- (H) We are visit my Aunt Ruth, too.
- (J) Correct as it is

5. Which of the following is not a sentence?

- (A) Sentence 1
- (B) Sentence 3
- (C) Sentence 4
- (D) Sentence 7

GO

Name _____   Date _____

Sample Test 5: Usage

Directions: Read each item. Choose the sentence that is written correctly.

6. (F) Them biscuits we baked were terrible.

   (G) Even the dog won't eat them.

   (H) When I dropping one, it made a loud noise.

   (J) I are not sure that we can eat them.

7. (A) I could had done those problems.

   (B) Didn't need help.

   (C) I listened carefully in class.

   (D) I knowed how to do them.

8. (F) The campers watched in horror as the bear took their food.

   (G) Scrambled eggs, bacon, and juice.

   (H) The bear dranked all the juice last.

   (J) He did to like his breakfast that morning.

9. (A) Concert in the park last night.

   (B) Music, dancing, and cheering.

   (C) More than a thousand people was there.

   (D) I will never forget that concert.

Directions: Choose the best combination for each pair of sentences.

10. **Jack is late.**
    Jack has gotten lost.

    (F) Jack is late, and Jack has gotten lost.

    (G) Jack has gotten lost, and he is late.

    (H) Jack, gotten lost, is late.

    (J) Jack, is late, and has gotten lost.

11. **Ana is my best friend.**
    Ana is my cousin.

    (A) My best friend, Ana is my cousin.

    (B) My cousin Ana, Ana is my best friend.

    (C) My cousin Ana is my best friend.

    (D) My best friend and cousin, Ana.

12. **Maggie is visiting her grandmother.**
    Maggie's grandmother lives in Arizona.

    (F) In Arizona, Maggie is visiting her grandmother.

    (G) Maggie is visiting Arizona and her grandmother.

    (H) Maggie's grandmother is being visited by Maggie in Arizona.

    (J) Maggie is visiting her grandmother in Arizona.

Sample Test 5: Usage

Directions: Read each paragraph. Choose the answer that is the best topic sentence for that paragraph.

13. **_____ First, I think it would be fun to spend some time with my friends. Second, we have not had a homemade cake in a long time. Third, my sister and brother would enjoy a birthday party, too.**

Ⓐ I would like to invite six friends.

Ⓑ I am turning nine in two weeks.

Ⓒ I would like a new computer game for my birthday.

Ⓓ I think I should be able to have a birthday party for three reasons.

14. **_____ Winter is white with snow. The cold air feels good on my face. I love building forts and making snow angels. I also love drinking hot chocolate in front of the fire.**

Ⓕ Winter is my favorite season.

Ⓖ In winter, you can go ice skating.

Ⓗ In some places, it doesn't snow in the winter.

Ⓙ I don't like winter.

15. **_____ Surfing and bike riding are her favorites, but she's good at lots of different sports. Trina won a championship in tennis, and she is also a good swimmer. In the winter, she likes to go skiing and skating.**

Ⓐ Trina is a good baseball player.

Ⓑ Trina is a good student.

Ⓒ Trina loves sports.

Ⓓ Trina won a swimming medal.

GO

Sample Test 5: Usage

Directions: Read the paragraph, and answer the questions that follow.

> **(1)** When the rocks were brought back to Earth, people studied them. **(2)** Many things about the moon. **(3)** One discovery was the age of the moon. **(4)** The rocks also told us that there is very little water on the moon.

16. Choose the best topic sentence for this paragraph.

(F) In the 1960s, there was a race to get to the moon.

(G) In 1969, three men landed on the moon.

(H) Neil Armstrong was the first man to step onto the moon's surface.

(J) In 1969, astronauts brought back rocks from the moon.

17. Choose the best last sentence for this paragraph.

(A) The first journey to the moon helped us learn more about our universe.

(B) The United States won the race to the moon.

(C) I wonder what the astronauts thought about the moon?

(D) The moon is very old.

18. Choose the best sentence to add between Sentences 3 and 4.

(F) The rocks from space were looked at in a lab.

(G) The moon rocks were very valuable.

(H) By studying the moon rocks, we learned more about the moon's soil.

(J) The astronauts kept some moon rocks for themselves.

19. Which choice is not a complete sentence?

(A) Sentence 1

(B) Sentence 2

(C) Sentence 3

(D) Sentence 4

Sample Test 5: Usage

Directions: Read each item, and choose the best answer.

20. Which word comes first in the dictionary?

- (F) this
- (G) thirty
- (H) thirsty
- (J) thirteen

21. Which word comes first in the dictionary?

- (A) tiger
- (B) tin
- (C) tiny
- (D) tine

22. Which word comes first in the dictionary?

- (F) arrow
- (G) ants
- (H) anteater
- (J) author

23. Which word comes first in the dictionary?

- (A) money
- (B) monkey
- (C) month
- (D) more

24. Look at the guide words. Which word would be found on the page?

| branch | | brown |

- (F) brute
- (G) broken
- (H) burn
- (J) brake

25. Look at the guide words. Which word would be found on the page?

| prize | | pump |

- (A) puppy
- (B) pet
- (C) protect
- (D) punish

26. Look at the guide words. Which word would be found on the page?

| strawberry | | stroll |

- (F) stress
- (G) strong
- (H) straw
- (J) strum

27. Look at the guide words. Which word would be found on the page?

| sheet | | shirt |

- (A) short
- (B) shread
- (C) shut
- (D) shin

GO

Sample Test 5: Usage

Directions: Read each question, and choose the best answer.

28. Where would you look to find the date of Memorial Day this year?

(F) in a newspaper

(G) in a catalog

(H) in a dictionary

(J) on a calendar

29. Which of these books would help you find out about becoming a pilot?

(A) *The History of Flight*

(B) *Finding the Cheapest Airfares*

(C) *Learning to Fly and Navigate*

(D) *The Flight to the North Pole*

Directions: Use the table of contents to answer the following questions.

TABLE OF CONTENTS

Chapter 1: Choosing Your Breed of Dog 11
Chapter 2: Selecting the Right Puppy 42
Chapter 3: Care and Feeding of Puppies 58
Chapter 4: Training Young Dogs 86
Chapter 5: Medical Care for Dogs 102
Chapter 6: Do You Have a Champion? 116

30. To learn how to teach your dog to sit, turn to _____.

(F) Chapter 1

(G) Chapter 2

(H) Chapter 3

(J) Chapter 4

31. A good title for this book might be _____.

(A) *The Dog Owner's Manual*

(B) *Finding a Puppy of Your Own*

(C) *Champion Dog Breeds*

(D) *The History of Pets*

32. If your puppy seems to have a cold, turn to page _____.

(F) 42

(G) 58

(H) 86

(J) 102

33. If you can't decide what kind of dog you want, turn to _____.

(A) Chapter 1

(B) Chapter 2

(C) Chapter 3

(D) Chapter 4

STOP

Understanding Point of View

Directions: Read the passages, and answer the questions.

A Sad Tale

A. I felt sorry for Jason when I saw him come in this morning. He looked so sad. When it was finally time for recess, I asked him to stay behind. Then, he told me his problem. With one quick phone call, the problem was solved.

B. I was in such a rush this morning, I forgot my lunch. Mom had packed an extra treat today. At recess, Ms. Warner asked me what was wrong. Then, she made a phone call, and Mom soon brought my lunch.

C. As soon as Jason left for the bus, I saw his lunch sitting on the counter. I had planned to bring it to school anyway, but I was glad that Ms. Warner called. Jason was so happy to get the extra treat I had packed for him.

I. **Who is the writer of passage A?**

_____

_____

How does this person help?

_____

_____

2. Who is the writer of passage B?

_____

_____

What is this person's main problem?

_____

_____

3. Who is the writer of passage C?

_____

_____

How does this person help?

_____

_____

4. What is being described in all three passages?

_____

_____

_____

Selecting Writing Formats

Directions: Read the paragraph about one student's favorite class. Then, write sentences to answer each question about your favorite class.

My favorite class is art. I like to draw and paint. Mr. Clausen is so nice and helpful. He shows us how to do new things, like make collages and clay sculptures. I always look forward to art class. Actually, it would be even better if it were longer!

1. What is your favorite class?

_____

_____

_____

_____

_____

2. Why is it your favorite?

_____

_____

_____

_____

_____

_____

3. Choose one of the following forms of writing—poem, story, or letter—to describe your ideas and feelings about your favorite class. Identify who your audience will be before writing.

_____

_____

_____

_____

_____

_____

_____

_____

If you have the time, go back and reread your answers to look for mistakes.

Writing with Organization

Directions: Write a paragraph about one of your favorite activities. Make sure your paragraph has a main idea and details that support the main idea. Use the chart below to create a rough draft of your paragraph. Then, write the final paragraph on the lines below.

Main Idea: _____

Detail 1: _____

Detail 2: _____

Detail 3: _____

Detail 4: _____

Conclusion: _____

_____

_____

_____

_____

_____

_____

_____

_____

_____

_____

_____

_____

Beginnings, Middles, and Ends

Directions: Read the passage, and answer the questions.

Insects in Winter

(1) In the summertime, insects buzz and flutter all around. But as winter's cold weather begins, the insects seem to disappear. Do you know where they go? Many insects find a warm place to spend the winter.

(2) Ants try to dig deep into the ground. Some beetles stack up in piles under rocks or dead leaves.

(3) Female grasshoppers don't even stay around for winter. In the fall, they lay their eggs and die. The eggs hatch in the spring.

(4) Bees also try to protect themselves from the winter cold. Honeybees gather in a ball in the middle of their hive. The bees stay in this tight ball trying to stay warm.

(5) Winter is very hard for insects. Each spring the survivors come out, and the buzzing and fluttering begins again.

1. Which paragraph is the beginning?

- (A) 1
- (B) 2
- (C) 3
- (D) 5

2. Which paragraph is the conclusion?

- (F) 1
- (G) 2
- (H) 4
- (J) 5

3. Use the passage to fill in the topic sentence below. Fill in the rest of the ovals with supporting details.

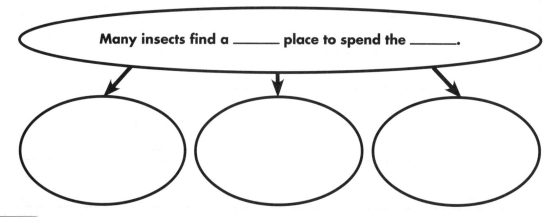

Many insects find a _____ place to spend the _____.

Using Writing Structures

Directions: Read the paragraph that tells how to make a peanut butter and jelly sandwich. Then, think of something you like to make or do. Write a paragraph about it. Use words like *first*, *next*, *then*, and *last* to show the order of the steps.

These steps tell how to make a peanut butter and jelly sandwich. First, get two pieces of bread, peanut butter, jelly, and a knife. Next, spread peanut butter on one piece of bread. Then, spread jelly on the other piece. Last, press the two pieces of bread together.

_____

_____

_____

_____

_____

_____

_____

_____

_____

_____

_____

_____

Using Writing Structures

Directions: Read the paragraph below about how to make a peanut butter and jelly sandwich. Notice that the steps are now numbered. In the space below, rewrite your directions from page 107. This time, use numbered steps instead of transitional words.

These steps tell how to make a peanut butter and jelly sandwich.
1. Get two pieces of bread, peanut butter, jelly, and a knife.
2. Spread peanut butter on one piece of bread.
3. Spread jelly on the other piece.
4. Press the two pieces of bread together.

_____

_____

_____

_____

_____

_____

_____

_____

_____

_____

_____

_____

_____

_____

Sample Test 6: Writing

Directions: Read the question, and write your answer.

What genre or type of writing do you like best? Explain your answer. (Some examples of different genres are biography, poetry, fable, and nonfiction.)

_____

_____

_____

_____

_____

_____

_____

_____

_____

_____

_____

_____

_____

_____

_____

GO

Sample Test 6: Writing

Directions: Read each item, and write your answer.

1. Write a paragraph about something you hope to do next summer. Make sure to include a main idea, details, and a conclusion.

_____

_____

_____

_____

_____

_____

_____

_____

2. Write a short paragraph that explains how to do something. Be sure to include words such as *first*, *next*, and *last*.

_____

_____

_____

_____

_____

_____

STOP

Practice Test 2: Language
Part 1: Mechanics

Directions: Choose the answer that shows the missing punctuation mark. If no punctuation is missing, choose "None."

1. Is that your house

- (A) .
- (B) ?
- (C) !
- (D) None

2. Mr Sanchez is a lawyer.

- (F) .
- (G) ,
- (H) !
- (J) None

3. Don't touch that

- (A) ?
- (B) ,
- (C) !
- (D) None

4. The old dog slept in the sun.

- (F) .
- (G) ,
- (H) !
- (J) None

5. We moved here from Tallahassee Florida.

- (A) .
- (B) ,
- (C) !
- (D) None

Directions: Choose the answer that shows the correct punctuation for the missing word.

6. _____ you Ethan's cousin?

- (F) Aren't
- (G) Arent
- (H) Are'nt
- (J) Arent'

7. _____ walk on the grass.

- (A) Dont
- (B) Don't
- (C) Dont'
- (D) Do'nt

8. _____ better at math than I am.

- (F) Youre
- (G) Your'e
- (H) Youre'
- (J) You're

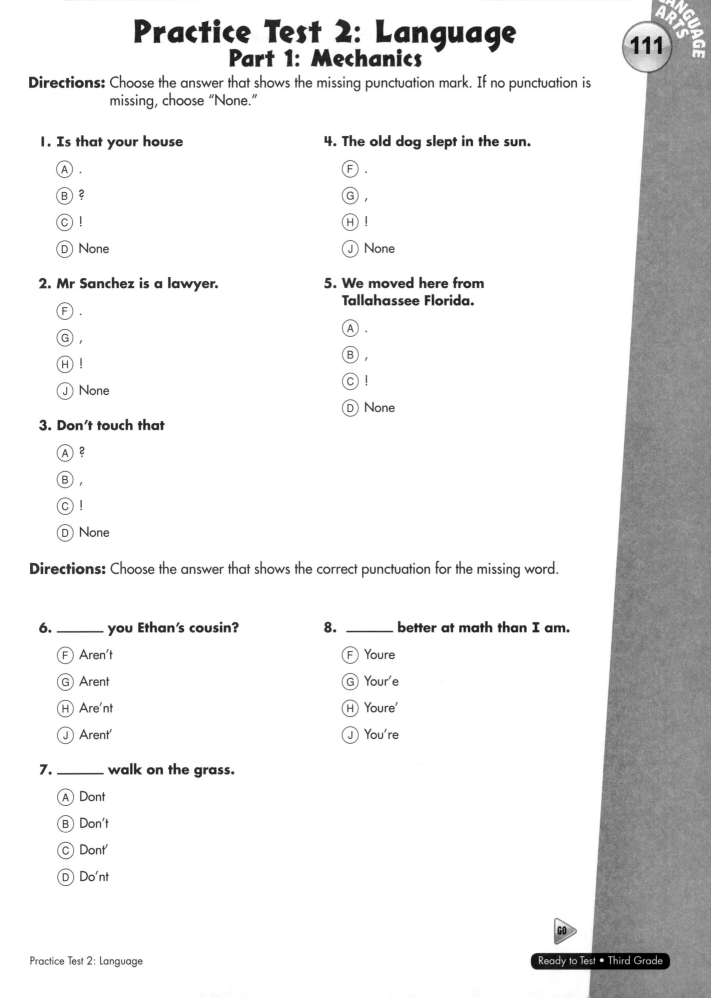

GO

Practice Test 2: Language
Part 1: Mechanics

Directions: Choose the answer in which a capital letter is missing. If no capital letters are missing, choose "None."

9. (A) he walked
(B) to the store
(C) to buy milk.
(D) None

10. (F) My aunt
(G) is named
(H) aunt Tilly.
(J) None

11. (A) On our trip
(B) to France,
(C) we saw Roman ruins.
(D) None

12. (F) My mother
(G) wrote a book called
(H) *The ocean and You.*
(J) None

13. (A) My brothers
(B) are named
(C) Jared and Jamal.
(D) None

Directions: Choose the answer that shows the correct capitalization.

14. Did you start school on _____?
(F) tuesday morning
(G) Tuesday morning
(H) Tuesday Morning
(J) tuesday Morning

15. Ms. Wu is my _____.
(A) favorite teacher
(B) Favorite teacher
(C) favorite Teacher
(D) Favorite Teacher

16. Isn't that zoo in _____?
(F) San francisco
(G) San Francisco
(H) san francisco
(J) san Francisco

17. Science is my _____.
(A) best Subject
(B) Best Subject
(C) Best subject
(D) best subject

GO

Practice Test 2: Language
Part 1: Mechanics

Directions: Read the passage. Then, answer the questions about the underlined phrases. Choose "Correct as it is" if the underlined part of the sentence is correct.

---

(1) <u>Yellowstone park</u> is known for its geysers. (2) A geyser is formed when water is trapped under the <u>ground melted rock</u> heats the water. (3) When the water boils, it shoots through a hole and high into the air. (4) <u>There are more than 300 geysers in Yellowstone.</u> (5) The best-known geyser is called <u>old faithful</u>. (6) It is as faithful as a clock. (7) <u>Old Faithfuls fame</u> makes it the most visited geyser in Yellowstone Park.

---

18. In Sentence 1, <u>Yellowstone park</u> is best written _____.

- (F) yellowstone park
- (G) Yellowstone Park
- (H) YellowStone Park
- (J) Correct as it is

19. In Sentence 2, <u>ground melted rock</u> is best written _____.

- (A) ground. Melted rock
- (B) ground, melted rock
- (C) ground melted. Rock
- (D) Correct as it is

20. In Sentence 4, <u>There are more than 300 geysers in Yellowstone.</u> is best written _____.

- (F) There are More than 300 geysers in Yellowstone.
- (G) There are more than 300 geysers. In Yellowstone.
- (H) There are more than 300 geysers in yellowstone.
- (J) Correct as it is

21. In Sentence 5, <u>old faithful</u> is best written _____.

- (A) old Faithful
- (B) Old faithful
- (C) Old Faithful
- (D) Correct as it is

22. In Sentence 7, <u>Old Faithfuls fame</u> is best written _____.

- (F) Old Faithfuls' fame
- (G) old Faithful's fame
- (H) Old Faithful's fame
- (J) Correct as it is

GO

Name _____ Date _____

Practice Test 2: Language
Part 1: Mechanics

Directions: For each item, choose the word that fits into the sentence and is spelled correctly.

23. He shot the _____ into the air.

Ⓐ arrow

Ⓑ errow

Ⓒ airrow

Ⓓ airow

24. Do you _____ your seatbelt?

Ⓕ fastin

Ⓖ fassen

Ⓗ fastain

Ⓙ fasten

25. Vijay has a new _____.

Ⓐ wissel

Ⓑ whistill

Ⓒ whistle

Ⓓ wistle

26. Sabrina wouldn't _____ to do that!

Ⓕ dare

Ⓖ dair

Ⓗ daire

Ⓙ dere

27. The cord would not _____ that far.

Ⓐ strech

Ⓑ stretch

Ⓒ stretsh

Ⓓ streitch

Directions: Choose the word that is spelled incorrectly. If all the words are spelled correctly, choose "No mistakes."

28. Ⓕ public

Ⓖ prepair

Ⓗ frown

Ⓙ No mistakes

29. Ⓐ suffer

Ⓑ pleasure

Ⓒ pleasant

Ⓓ No mistakes

30. Ⓕ imagene

Ⓖ marry

Ⓗ court

Ⓙ No mistakes

31. Ⓐ toughest

Ⓑ principal

Ⓒ emergensy

Ⓓ No mistakes

Practice Test 2: Language
Part 1: Mechanics

Directions: For each item, choose the word that is spelled correctly.

32. (F) beaf
(G) cideer
(H) cheif
(J) miracle

33. (A) graduete
(B) strayt
(C) solar
(D) calandar

34. (F) mayor
(G) honer
(H) experiance
(J) dekorate

35. (A) enough
(B) releese
(C) foldar
(D) tuff

36. (F) villaje
(G) diskuss
(H) contast
(J) squirrel

37. (A) wherevar
(B) prisaner
(C) blendar
(D) invitation

38. (F) babys
(G) sneekers
(H) product
(J) progrem

39. (A) iland
(B) melan
(C) humid
(D) dutys

40. (F) sprinkle
(G) posishun
(H) gymasium
(J) billyan

Directions: Read each sentence. Choose the underlined word that is spelled incorrectly. Choose "No mistakes" if the entire sentence is correct.

41. (A) The hidden <u>passege</u>
(B) was <u>flooded</u>
(C) with <u>freezing</u> water.
(D) No mistakes

42. (F) The quiet <u>village</u>
(G) was <u>destroied</u>
(H) by the <u>giant</u>.
(J) No mistakes

43. (A) The <u>engine</u>
(B) has <u>stopped</u>
(C) on the <u>mountain</u>.
(D) No mistakes

44. (F) It seems a <u>shame</u>
(G) to <u>waist</u>
(H) such a <u>beautiful</u> day.
(J) No mistakes

Name _____   Date _____

Practice Test 2: Language
Part 2: Grammar

Directions: Read each item. Choose the word that best completes the sentence.

1. **Please lend _____ your mittens.**

   Ⓐ her

   Ⓑ she

   Ⓒ its

   Ⓓ they

2. **Don't _____ in the hallway.**

   Ⓕ running

   Ⓖ ran

   Ⓗ run

   Ⓙ had run

3. **The vine _____ up the side of the house.**

   Ⓐ climbing

   Ⓑ climbs

   Ⓒ did climbing

   Ⓓ climb

4. **Dr. and Mrs. Santiago _____ the school last Monday.**

   Ⓕ visiting

   Ⓖ visit

   Ⓗ visits

   Ⓙ visited

Directions: Choose the answer that is a correct and complete sentence.

5. Ⓐ Basketball was first thinked up by a teacher.

   Ⓑ He needed a game for students to play indoors in the winter.

   Ⓒ He nails a basket to the ball and made up a set of rules.

   Ⓓ I think him had an idea that we can all enjoy!

6. Ⓕ Bird watchers sometimes see birds taking dust baths.

   Ⓖ The birds use the dust like them bathtub.

   Ⓗ The dust helps they get rid of tiny bugs in their feathers.

   Ⓙ The birds is smart to do this.

7. Ⓐ Sunflowers can be up to a foot wide.

   Ⓑ It's petals are yellow.

   Ⓒ They stem of this flower is very tall.

   Ⓓ Some sunflowers is twice as tall as children.

GO

Name _____ Date _____

Practice Test 2: Language
Part 2: Grammar

Directions: Choose the answer in which the simple subject of the sentence is underlined.

8. (F) The brave <u>firefighters</u> are always ready to go.

   (G) A loud <u>bell</u> rings.

   (H) The <u>firefighters</u> get into their red truck.

   (J) A spotted <u>dog</u> runs behind.

9. (A) <u>I</u> like to take care of my garden.

   (B) The black <u>crows</u> want to eat my corn.

   (C) The little <u>rabbit</u> wants to eat my carrots.

   (D) Even <u>my silly dog</u> likes to dig in the garden.

10. (F) My best <u>friend</u>, Ed, likes to play baseball.

   (G) My two <u>cousins</u> like to play, too.

   (H) <u>We</u> play on a team together.

   (J) The baseball <u>games</u> start next week.

11. (A) The <u>Golden Gate Bridge</u> was built across a large bay.

   (B) Two <u>towers</u> hold up the bridge.

   (C) Giant <u>cables</u> hang between the towers.

   (D) This special <u>bridge</u> is famous.

12. (F) <u>People</u> built bridges long ago, just like they do today.

   (G) One kind of <u>bridge</u> was called a *rope bridge*.

   (H) The <u>Romans</u> built some stone bridges.

   (J) All kinds of <u>bridges</u> helped people in their daily lives.

Directions: Choose the answer choice that has the mistake. If all choices are correct, choose "No mistakes."

13. (A) The running shoes

   (B) wasn't the right size,

   (C) so I returned them.

   (D) No mistakes

14. (F) A baby kangaroo

   (G) lives in its mothers pouch

   (H) for nine months.

   (J) No mistakes

15. (A) Josh ran back

   (B) to mason Park

   (C) to look for his gloves.

   (D) No mistakes

16. (F) I was worried

   (G) that I did badly

   (H) on the history test.

   (J) No mistakes

STOP

Practice Test 2: Language
Part 3: Usage

Directions: Choose the best combination for each pair of sentences.

1. Angelo went downtown.
Angelo went to the store.

(A) Angelo went to the store and Angelo went downtown.

(B) Angelo went to the store and downtown.

(C) Angelo, who went downtown, went to the store.

(D) Angelo went downtown to the store.

2. Mr. Lee is my teacher.
Mr. Lee teaches third grade.

(F) Mr. Lee teaches third grade, and he is my teacher.

(G) Mr. Lee is my teacher and he teaches third grade.

(H) Mr. Lee is my teacher for third grade.

(J) Mr. Lee, teaches third grade, is my teacher.

3. You may play outside.
You may play after you clean your room.

(A) After you clean your room, you may play outside.

(B) You may play outside, but you may play after you clean your room.

(C) You may play after you clean your room, outside.

(D) Playing outside, you may after you clean your room.

Directions: Choose the best version of each sentence.

4. (F) On the hill, Mr. Juarez lives in the house with the big garden.

(G) Mr. Juarez lives in the house with the big garden, on the hill.

(H) Mr. Juarez lives in the house on the hill with the big garden.

(J) With the big garden, Mr. Juarez lives in the house on the hill.

5. (A) On Saturday, we went to Grant Park for a picnic.

(B) To Grant Park we went, on Saturday, for a picnic.

(C) We went, for a picnic, to grant Park on Saturday.

(D) For a picnic, we went on Saturday to Grant Park.

Practice Test 2: Language
Part 3: Usage

Directions: Read the selection, and answer the questions that follow.

(1) Snowflakes look like white stars falling from the sky. (2) But there have been times when snow has looked red, green, yellow, and even black. (3) Black snow in France one year. (4) Another year, gray snow fell in Japan. (5) To make this dark snow, snow had mixed with ashes to make it. (6) Red snow that fell one year was made of snow mixed with red clay dust. (7) Most snow looks white. (8) It is really the color of ice. (9) Each snowflake begins with a small drop of frozen water. (10) When that water is mixed with some other material, the result is strangely-colored snow.

6. Sentence 5 is best written

F) Snow had mixed with ashes to make this dark snow.

G) Snow mixed with ashes was how this snow was made into dark snow.

H) To make this dark snow, it had ashes mixed in with it.

J) Correct as it is

7. Which is not a complete sentence?

A) Sentence 1

B) Sentence 2

C) Sentence 3

D) Sentence 4

8. How could Sentences 7 and 8 best be joined together?

F) Really the color of ice, most snow looks white.

G) The color of ice, most snow is really white.

H) Most snow looks white and it is really the color of ice.

J) Most snow looks white, but it is really the color of ice.

9. Choose a topic sentence for this paragraph.

A) Imagine what it would be like to have colored snowflakes coming down around you.

B) Black snow in France scared the citizens.

C) Snow is always white, but it is really the color of ice.

D) Drops of frozen water make snow.

GO

Practice Test 2: Language
Part 3: Usage

Directions: Read each question, and choose the best answer.

10. Which word comes first in the dictionary?

(F) slipper

(G) slink

(H) slip

(J) slim

11. Which word comes first in the dictionary?

(A) interesting

(B) indeed

(C) insurance

(D) idea

12. Which word comes first in the dictionary?

(F) lettuce

(G) let

(H) lean

(J) leak

13. Which word comes first in the dictionary?

(A) cheese

(B) chess

(C) cheat

(D) chalk

14. Where would you look to find out how to break *yesterday* into syllables?

(F) in a newspaper

(G) in a history book

(H) in a dictionary

(J) in an online encyclopedia

15. Where would you look to find a map of Oregon?

(A) in a newspaper

(B) in an atlas

(C) in a telephone book

(D) in a math book

16. Where would you look to find the address and telephone number of a restaurant?

(F) in a newspaper

(G) online

(H) in a dictionary

(J) in an encyclopedia

17. Look at the guide words. Which word would be found on the page?

| part | | pet |

(A) petticoat

(B) pen

(C) pair

(D) pardon

18. Look at the guide words. Which word would be found on the page?

| mint | | mist |

(F) minute

(G) minnow

(H) misty

(J) mysterious

Practice Test 2: Language
Part 3: Usage

Directions: Use the index below to answer the questions that follow.

O

Oak,	291–292
Obsidian,	175–176
Oceans,	361–375
density in,	363–364
temperatures of,	365
life in,	367–370
waves,	371–372
resources,	373–375

19. On what pages would you find information about oak trees?

Ⓐ pages 175–176
Ⓑ pages 291–292
Ⓒ pages 361–375
Ⓓ pages 376–399

20. What information will you find on page 365?

Ⓕ ocean temperatures
Ⓖ density of the ocean
Ⓗ waves
Ⓙ ocean life

21. On what pages will you find out about mining in the ocean for minerals?

Ⓐ pages 175–176
Ⓑ pages 368–369
Ⓒ pages 373–375
Ⓓ pages 371–372

22. You can read about octopuses on pages 368–369. In which section of Oceans is this?

Ⓕ resources
Ⓖ life in
Ⓗ waves
Ⓙ temperatures

Directions: Use the dictionary entry to answer the questions that follow.

beam [bēm] *n.* 1. a squared-off log used to support a building 2. a ray of light 3. the wooden roller in a loom *v.* 1. to shine 2. to smile broadly

23. In which sentence is *beam* used as a verb?

Ⓐ The beam held up the plaster ceiling.
Ⓑ The beam of light warmed the room.
Ⓒ She moved the beam before she added a row of wool.
Ⓓ The children beam in the photo.

24. Which sentence uses *beam* as in the first definition of the noun?

Ⓕ The ceiling beam fell into the room.
Ⓖ The beam of the loom was broken.
Ⓗ She beamed her approval.
Ⓙ The beam of sunlight came through the tree.

Practice Test 2: Language
Part 4: Writing

Directions: Read each item, and write your answer.

1. Write a short paragraph from your own point of view.

_____

_____

_____

_____

_____

_____

_____

2. Now, rewrite the paragraph from someone else's point of view.

_____

_____

_____

_____

_____

_____

_____

STOP

Number Sense

Name _____ **Date** _____

Directions: Read each problem. Find the correct answer. Fill in the circle.

Example

The number 589 is less than _____.

- (A) 598
- (B) 579
- (C) 589
- (D) 588

Answer: (A)

---

4. If you arranged these numbers from least to greatest, which number would be last?

| 3,312 | 3,302 | 3,213 | 3,012 |

- (F) 3,312
- (G) 3,302
- (H) 3,213
- (J) 3,012

1. You are ninth in line for movie tickets. How many people are ahead of you?

- (A) 9
- (B) 7
- (C) 8
- (D) 10

5. Which circle below shows $\frac{3}{4}$?

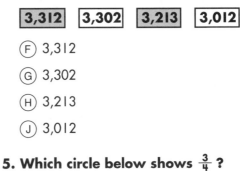

- (A)
- (B)
- (C)
- (D)

2. Which number is greater than 97?

- (F) 55
- (G) 102
- (H) 87
- (J) 96

3. How many of these numbers are greater than 218?

| 222 | 245 | 212 | 245 |

- (A) 1
- (B) 2
- (C) 3
- (D) 4

Name _____ Date _____

Number Sense

Directions: Read each problem. Find the correct answer. Fill in the circle.

1. **Count by tens. Which number comes after 70 and before 90?**
   - (A) 50
   - (B) 60
   - (C) 80
   - (D) 100

2. **The number 5,066 is greater than _____.**
   - (F) 5,069
   - (G) 6,065
   - (H) 5,062
   - (J) 5,099

3. **If you arranged these numbers from greatest to least, which number would be last?**

   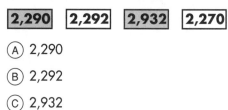

   - (A) 2,290
   - (B) 2,292
   - (C) 2,932
   - (D) 2,270

4. **Which number is missing from the sequence?**

   - (F) 20
   - (G) 24
   - (H) 22
   - (J) 26

5. **Which of these fractions is the largest?**
   - (A) $\frac{2}{3}$
   - (B) $\frac{5}{6}$
   - (C) $\frac{1}{4}$
   - (D) $\frac{1}{6}$

6. **The number 422 is less than _____.**
   - (F) 412
   - (G) 442
   - (H) 421
   - (J) 402

7. **Count by fives. Which number comes after 35 and before 45?**
   - (A) 30
   - (B) 40
   - (C) 25
   - (D) 50

8. **The number 2,256 is less than _____.**
   - (F) 2,250
   - (G) 1,926
   - (H) 2,200
   - (J) 2,270

Name _____ Date _____

Number Sense

Directions: Read each problem. Find the correct answer. Fill in the circle.

1. How many of these numbers are greater than 2,665?

| 2,662 | 2,669 | 2,640 | 2,671 |

- Ⓐ 0
- Ⓑ 1
- Ⓒ 2
- Ⓓ 3

2. The number 1,691 is less than _____.

- Ⓕ 1,609
- Ⓖ 1,699
- Ⓗ 1,690
- Ⓙ 1,600

3. You are fourteenth in line at an amusement park. How many people are in line ahead of you?

- Ⓐ 14
- Ⓑ 16
- Ⓒ 13
- Ⓓ 12

4. Which number is missing from the sequence?

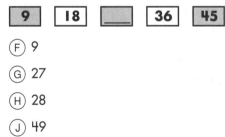

- Ⓕ 9
- Ⓖ 27
- Ⓗ 28
- Ⓙ 49

5. Lena needs a piece of wood that is between 3.55 and 4.20 inches long. Which piece of wood below could she use?

- Ⓐ 3.25 inches
- Ⓑ 3.98 inches
- Ⓒ 4.35 inches
- Ⓓ 4.40 inches

6. Which picture shows 24 flowers?

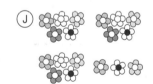

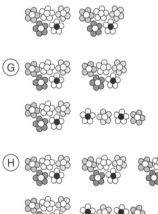

Number Sense

Directions: Read each problem. Find the correct answer. Fill in the circle.

1. Which number belongs in the box on the number line?

27 30 ☐ 40

- Ⓐ 34
- Ⓑ 36
- Ⓒ 38
- Ⓓ 40

2. Count by fives. Which number comes after 145 and before 155?

- Ⓕ 140
- Ⓖ 145
- Ⓗ 150
- Ⓙ 155

3. Which series shows the numbers in order from greatest to least?

- Ⓐ 98, 77, 74, 39, 32, 18, 5
- Ⓑ 55, 57, 62, 68, 70, 71, 72
- Ⓒ 116, 122, 129, 185, 192, 215, 231
- Ⓓ 2, 4, 6, 8, 10, 12, 14

4. All of the Lewis children are between 33 and 48 inches tall. Which of the following cannot be the height of one of the Lewis children?

- Ⓕ 40 inches
- Ⓖ 37 inches
- Ⓗ 46 inches
- Ⓙ 31 inches

5. Which decimal is equal to $\frac{1}{4}$?

- Ⓐ 0.25
- Ⓑ 0.025
- Ⓒ 0.75
- Ⓓ 0.033

6. How many of these numbers are greater than 142?

180 140 124 147

- Ⓕ 1
- Ⓖ 2
- Ⓗ 3
- Ⓙ 4

If you have to guess, first get rid of any answer choices you know are incorrect.

Name _____ Date _____

Number Sense

Directions: Read each problem. Find the correct answer. Fill in the circle.

1.

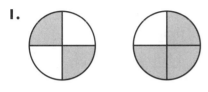

From the figures above, you know that

- (A) $\frac{1}{3}$ is greater than $\frac{2}{3}$.
- (B) $\frac{1}{2}$ is greater than $\frac{3}{4}$.
- (C) $\frac{1}{2}$ is greater than $\frac{1}{4}$.
- (D) $\frac{3}{4}$ is greater than $\frac{1}{2}$.

2. If you arranged these numbers from least to greatest, which number would be last?

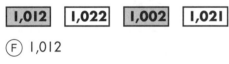

- (F) 1,012
- (G) 1,021
- (H) 1,022
- (J) 1,002

3. Which of these numbers would come after 8.6 on a number line?

- (A) 8.2
- (B) 6.8
- (C) 8.9
- (D) 8.0

4. Find the answer that shows 35 peanuts.

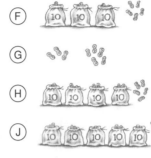

5. 0.5 =

- (A) $\frac{5}{0}$
- (B) $\frac{5}{100}$
- (C) $\frac{5}{10}$
- (D) $\frac{50}{10}$

6. Which amount is the same as 25 cents?

- (F) $\frac{3}{4}$ dollar
- (G) $\frac{1}{4}$ dollar
- (H) $\frac{1}{2}$ dollar
- (J) $\frac{2}{3}$ dollar

Look at any pictures or graphs carefully!

Number Sense

Directions: Read each problem. Find the correct answer. Fill in the circle.

1. **Which of these shows the same number of cats and dogs?**

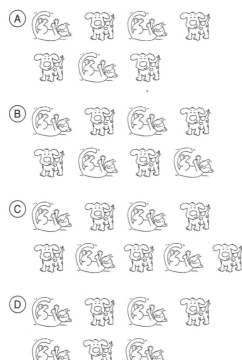

2. **Which of these numbers would come before 241 on a number line?**

    (F) 242
    (G) 260
    (H) 240
    (J) 244

3. **Count by tens. Which number comes after 30 and before 50?**

    (A) 20
    (B) 40
    (C) 60
    (D) 70

4. **How many of these numbers are greater than 1,114?**

    (F) 1
    (G) 2
    (H) 3
    (J) 4

5. **If a day's snowfall was between 1.01 inches and 2.32 inches, which of the measurements below might be the actual snowfall amount?**

    (A) 1.00 inch
    (B) 2.60 inches
    (C) 2.52 inches
    (D) 2.23 inches

6. **Which of these numbers would come before 92 on a number line?**

    (F) 90
    (G) 95
    (H) 104
    (J) 99

7. **How many of these numbers are greater than 565?**

    (A) 1
    (B) 2
    (C) 3
    (D) 4

Number Sense

Directions: Read each problem. Find the correct answer. Fill in the circle.

1. 0.8 =

(A) $\frac{1}{8}$

(B) $\frac{8}{100}$

(C) $\frac{80}{100}$

(D) $\frac{8}{10}$

2. Half a dollar is the same as _____.

(F) 25 cents

(G) 50 cents

(H) 75 cents

(J) $1.00

3. Which of these numbers would come before 157 on a number line?

(A) 159

(B) 147

(C) 165

(D) 158

4. How much of the circle below is shaded?

(F) $\frac{5}{6}$

(G) $\frac{2}{3}$

(H) $\frac{1}{2}$

(J) $\frac{1}{6}$

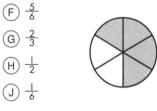

5. Which number belongs in the box on the number line?

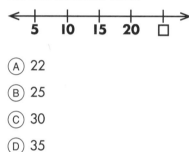

(A) 22

(B) 25

(C) 30

(D) 35

6. Which number is missing from the sequence?

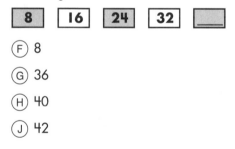

(F) 8

(G) 36

(H) 40

(J) 42

Name _____   Date _____

Number Sense

Directions: Read each problem. Find the correct answer. Fill in the circle.

1. From the picture, you can tell that _____.

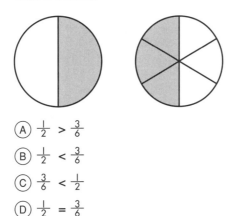

- (A) $\frac{1}{2} > \frac{3}{6}$
- (B) $\frac{1}{2} < \frac{3}{6}$
- (C) $\frac{3}{6} < \frac{1}{2}$
- (D) $\frac{1}{2} = \frac{3}{6}$

2. Gabe will meet his parents at the library between 4:15 and 4:35. At which of the following times might his parents arrive?

- (F) 4:12
- (G) 4:45
- (H) 4:27
- (J) 4:50

3. Which number is missing from the sequence?

- (A) 36
- (B) 12
- (C) 32
- (D) 40

4. Which picture shows 17 pencils?

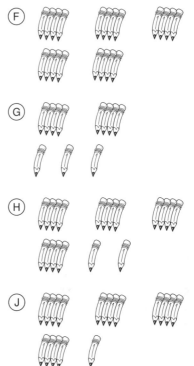

5. Which decimal is equal to $\frac{3}{4}$?

- (A) 0.75
- (B) 0.075
- (C) 0.34
- (D) 0.25

6. Which number sentence is not true?

- (F) $\frac{4}{8} = \frac{1}{2}$
- (G) $\frac{1}{2} = \frac{1}{4}$
- (H) $\frac{2}{3} = \frac{4}{6}$
- (J) $\frac{2}{3} > \frac{1}{3}$

Number Sense

Directions: Read each problem. Find the correct answer. Fill in the circle.

1. **Which number is greater than 600 and has a 4 in the tens place?**

   (A) 342

   (B) 904

   (C) 846

   (D) 454

2. **Which number is between 2,000 and 3,000?**

   (F) 1,980

   (G) 3,200

   (H) 3,001

   (J) 2,589

3. **Which number is less than 1,000 and has a 5 in the ones place?**

   (A) 853

   (B) 5

   (C) 540

   (D) 1,065

4. **Which number is between 150 and 250 and is made of all even numbers?**

   (F) 144

   (G) 286

   (H) 228

   (J) 229

5. **Which number is less than 2?**

   (A) 2.14

   (B) 2.22

   (C) 1.89

   (D) 3.46

6. **Which number is even and has a 6 in the thousands place?**

   (F) 6,574

   (G) 6,881

   (H) 5,632

   (J) 6,667

7. **Which number is between 800 and 900?**

   (A) 799

   (B) 901

   (C) 898

   (D) 999

8. **Which number is between 400 and 500 and is made of all even numbers?**

   (F) 504

   (G) 424

   (H) 499

   (J) 450

Number Concepts

Directions: Read and work each problem. Find the correct answer. Fill in the circle.

Example

Which number makes this number sentence true?

$50 - \square = 24$

- (A) 36
- (B) 26
- (C) 16
- (D) 24

Answer: (B)

---

1. Which number makes this number sentence true?

$\square \times 4 = 8$

- (A) 1
- (B) 2
- (C) 0
- (D) 4

2. Which number makes this number sentence true?

$\square \times 3 = 9$

- (F) 0
- (G) 2
- (H) 3
- (J) 4

3. Which number makes this number sentence true?

$\square \div 2 = 7$

- (A) 9
- (B) 5
- (C) 3
- (D) 14

4. Which number makes this number sentence true?

$\square - 37 = 53$

- (F) 100
- (G) 110
- (H) 90
- (J) 89

5. Which number makes this number sentence true?

$\square \div 4 = 51$

- (A) 204
- (B) 240
- (C) 47
- (D) 55

Read each question carefully.
If you are working on scrap paper, be sure to read your notes carefully, too.

Number Concepts

Directions: Read and work each problem. Find the correct answer. Fill in the circle.

1. Which number makes this number sentence true?

   $\square \times 3 = 15$

   (A) 5
   (B) 3
   (C) 4
   (D) 6

2. Which number makes this number sentence true?

   $\square + 22 = 30$

   (F) 7
   (G) 8
   (H) 9
   (J) 12

3. Which number makes this number sentence true?

   $50 - \square = 14$

   (A) 30
   (B) 26
   (C) 36
   (D) 14

4. Which number makes this number sentence true?

   $\square \div 5 = 4$

   (F) 25
   (G) 20
   (H) 18
   (J) 30

5. Which number makes this number sentence true?

   $13 \times \square = 130$

   (A) 10
   (B) 12
   (C) 5
   (D) 15

6. Which number makes this number sentence true?

   $\square + 16 = 74$

   (F) 55
   (G) 60
   (H) 48
   (J) 58

Number Concepts

MATH
134

Directions: Read and work each problem. Find the correct answer. Fill in the circle.

Example

12 + □ = 17
10 − □ = 5
Which number completes both number sentences?

- (A) 3
- (B) 6
- (C) 5
- (D) 7

Answer: C

---

1. 18 □ 9 = 9
Which operation sign belongs in the box?

- (A) +
- (B) −
- (C) ×
- (D) ÷

2. 22 + □ = 29
16 − □ = 9
Which number completes both number sentences?

- (F) 5
- (G) 9
- (H) 7
- (J) 6

3. Which image shows 8 − 4?

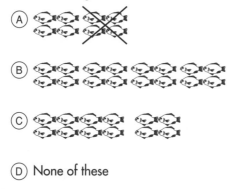

- (A)
- (B)
- (C)
- (D) None of these

4. 27 □ 8 = 19
10 □ 2 = 8
Which operation sign belongs in both boxes?

- (F) +
- (G) −
- (H) ×
- (J) ÷

5. Which number sentence shows how to find the total number of feathers?

- (A) 3 + 4
- (B) 3 ÷ 4
- (C) 4 − 3
- (D) 3 × 4

6. $\frac{1}{2} = \frac{3}{\square}$
What does the □ equal?

- (F) 2
- (G) 5
- (H) 4
- (J) 6

Number Concepts

Directions: Read and work each problem. Find the correct answer. Fill in the circle.

1. 6 □ 8 = 48
   4 □ 3 = 12
   Which operation sign belongs in both boxes?

   (A) +
   (B) −
   (C) ×
   (D) ÷

2. 49 □ 7 = 7
   Which operation sign belongs in the box?

   (F) +
   (G) −
   (H) ×
   (J) ÷

3. $\frac{4}{4}$ = □
   What does the □ equal?

   (A) 4
   (B) 1
   (C) $\frac{1}{2}$
   (D) $\frac{2}{4}$

4. **Which image shows 6 × 2?**

   (F) [fish image crossed out]

   (G) [fish images]

   (H) [fish images]

   (J) None of these

5. 25 □ 50 = 75
   18 □ 24 = 42
   Which operation sign belongs in both boxes?

   (A) +
   (B) −
   (C) ×
   (D) ÷

6. 99 □ 9 = 11
   Which operation sign belongs in the box?

   (F) +
   (G) −
   (H) ×
   (J) ÷

Are you sure that you know the right answer?

Mark it, and move on!

Number Concepts

Directions: The function machine uses rules to change numbers. Look for a pattern in the IN and OUT numbers in each table. Decide which function you need to use to get from each IN number to the OUT number below it. You will need to add, subtract, multiply, or divide. The same function and number is used for the entire table. Fill in the table. Then, write the rule for getting from the IN number to the OUT number.

Example

IN	3	8	13	19
OUT	5	10	_____	21

For this table, add 2 to each "in" number to find each "out" number. The missing number is 15. The rule is: Add 2.

1.

IN	78	15	41	22	37	_____	55
OUT	68	5	31	_____	_____	3	_____

Rule: _____

2.

IN	2	9	81	76	37	_____	_____
OUT	11	18	_____	85	_____	34	51

Rule: _____

3.

IN	12	16	30	34	44	_____	60
OUT	6	8	_____	_____	22	25	_____

Rule: _____

Number Concepts

Directions: Look for a pattern in the IN and OUT numbers in each table. Decide which function you need to use to get from each IN number to the OUT number below it. Fill in the table. Then, write the rule for getting from the IN number to the OUT number.

1.

IN	5	25	42	19	_____	59	12
OUT	10	30	47	_____	38	64	_____

Rule: _____

2.

IN	11	30	55	_____	16	29	88
OUT	19	_____	63	30	24	_____	96

Rule: _____

3.

IN	20	98	54	28	37	_____	8
OUT	18	96	_____	_____	35	53	6

Rule: _____

4.

IN	66	52	28	54	70	75	_____
OUT	46	_____	8	34	_____	55	70

Rule: _____

Number Concepts

Directions: Choose the equation that best describes the text. Fill in the circle.

Example

Izzy bought a smoothie for $3.25. She paid with a $5 bill. What is Izzy's change?

(A) $5.00 − $3.25 = ☐

(B) $3.25 − ☐ = $5.00

(C) $3.25 + $5.00 = ☐

(D) $3.25 × ☐ = $5.00

Answer: (A)

1. Mrs. Tram's class lines up in 6 equal lines. There are 24 students in her class. How many students are in each line?

(A) 6 × 24 = ☐

(B) 24 × ☐ = 6

(C) 6 + ☐ = 24

(D) 24 ÷ 6 = ☐

2. The park ranger sees 8 rabbits running into the woods. How many legs does she see?

(F) 8 + 4 = ☐

(G) 8 − 4 = ☐

(H) 8 × 4 = ☐

(J) 8 ÷ 4 = ☐

3. Darius's class is studying 11 different animals in science class. The class has 7 animals left to study. How many animals have they studied already?

(A) ☐ + 11 = 7

(B) 11 − 7 = ☐

(C) 11 + 7 = ☐

(D) ☐ − 7 = 11

4. For Kazuki's birthday, his mom made mini muffins for the class. There are 26 students in Kazuki's class. Each student will get 3 mini muffins. How many muffins did his mom make?

(F) ☐ × 3 = 26

(G) 26 ÷ 3 = ☐

(H) ☐ × 26 = 3

(J) 26 × 3 = ☐

Cover the answer choices, and read the problem. Think about your answer before you look at the choices. You'll be less likely to make a mistake!

Number Concepts

Directions: Choose the equation that best describes the text. Fill in the circle.

Look for key words and numbers that will help you find the answers.

1. There are 12 boys and girls on the softball team. They each need a new jersey and baseball cap. How many pieces of new gear does the team need?

- (A) $12 \div 2 = \square$
- (B) $12 \div \square = 2$
- (C) $12 \times 2 = \square$
- (D) $12 + 2 = \square$

2. Tasha delivers 56 papers every morning. She has delivered 14 so far today. How many does she still have in her basket?

- (F) $56 - 14 = \square$
- (G) $56 \div 14 = \square$
- (H) $56 \times \square = 14$
- (J) $14 - \square = 56$

3. Kate wants to buy a new notebook that costs $2.65 and a pack of colored pencils that cost $4.50. How much money does she need?

- (A) $\$4.50 - \$2.65 = \square$
- (B) $\$2.65 + \square = \$4.50$
- (C) $\$4.50 + \$2.65 = \square$
- (D) $\$4.50 \times \$2.65 = \square$

4. Mrs. Chavez has 88 water balloons. There are 22 students in her class. How many balloons will each student get?

- (F) $88 \times \square = 22$
- (G) $22 + \square = 88$
- (H) $88 \div 22 = \square$
- (J) $22 + 88 = \square$

5. It costs $0.19 to print a photo at the camera shop. How much does it cost to print 15 photos?

- (A) $\$0.19 \times 15 = \square$
- (B) $\$0.19 \div 15 = \square$
- (C) $\$0.19 + 15 = \square$
- (D) $\$0.19 \times \square = 15$

6. Liam walks 3 different dogs 5 days a week. How many dogs does Liam walk in a week?

- (F) $5 \div \square = 3$
- (G) $\square \times 3 = 5$
- (H) $3 + 5 = \square$
- (J) $3 \times 5 = \square$

MATH
140

Properties

Directions: Read each problem. Find the correct answer. Fill in the circle.

Example

What is another name for 72?

- (A) 7 tens and 3 ones
- (B) 8 tens and 0 ones
- (C) 7 tens and 7 ones
- (D) 7 tens and 2 ones

Answer: (D)

1. 7 thousands and 5 hundreds equals _____.

- (A) 5,700
- (B) 7,050
- (C) 570
- (D) 7,500

2. What is another name for 426?

- (F) 4 thousands, 2 tens, and 6 ones
- (G) 6 hundreds, 2 tens, and 4 ones
- (H) 2 tens and 6 ones
- (J) 4 hundreds, 2 tens, and 6 ones

3. What is another name for 4 hundreds, 6 tens, and 5 ones?

- (A) 4,650
- (B) 465
- (C) 40,650
- (D) 4,560

4. What is another name for 8 hundreds, 4 tens, and 3 ones?

- (F) 8,430
- (G) 843
- (H) 834
- (J) 8,043

5. 4 hundreds, 0 tens, and 6 ones equals _____.

- (A) 460
- (B) 406
- (C) 4,006
- (D) 4,060

6. How many thousands are in 6,517?

- (F) 5
- (G) 1
- (H) 6
- (J) 7

7. How many tens are in 3,280?

- (A) 0
- (B) 3
- (C) 8
- (D) 2

Properties

Directions: Read each problem. Find the correct answer. Fill in the circle.

1. What is another name for 5 hundreds, 9 tens, and 3 ones?

(A) 593

(B) 5,093

(C) 953

(D) 5,930

2. What is another name for 982?

(F) 9 thousands, 8 tens, and 2 ones

(G) 9 hundreds, 2 tens, and 8 ones

(H) 9 tens and 8 ones

(J) 9 hundreds, 8 tens, and 2 ones

3. Which of these is nine hundred sixty-four?

(A) 9,604

(B) 946

(C) 9,640

(D) 964

4. How many tens are in 5,743?

(F) 5

(G) 3

(H) 4

(J) 7

5. How many hundreds are in 2,931?

(A) 2

(B) 3

(C) 1

(D) 9

6. Which group of numbers has three even numbers?

(F) 6, 14, 23, 25, 33, 47, 55, 61

(G) 5, 17, 18, 21, 29, 30, 31, 44

(H) 11, 17, 25, 26, 33, 38, 49, 53

(J) 2, 7, 13, 29, 34, 37, 41, 45

Make sure you eat a good breakfast the morning of the test!

Properties

Name _____   Date _____

Directions: Read each problem. Find the correct answer. Fill in the circle.

1. How can you write 56,890 in expanded notation?

(A) $5 + 6 + 8 + 9 + 0$

(B) $50,000 + 6,000 + 800 + 90$

(C) $56,000 + 8,900$

(D) $0.5 + 0.06 + 0.008 + 0.0009$

2. What is another name for 651?

(F) 6 thousands, 5 tens, and 1 one

(G) 6 hundreds, 1 ten, and 5 ones

(H) 6 tens and 5 ones

(J) 6 hundreds, 5 tens, and 1 one

3. What number is represented by the chart?

Hundreds	Tens	Ones
I I I	I I I I I	I I I

(A) 335

(B) 533

(C) 353

(D) 335

4. How many hundreds are in 9,451?

(F) 9

(G) 4

(H) 5

(J) 1

5. How can you write 9,876 in expanded notation?

(A) $9,800 + 76 + 0$

(B) $9,800 + 70 + 60$

(C) $9,000 + 870 + 60$

(D) $9,000 + 800 + 70 + 6$

6. How many tens are in 60?

(F) 6

(G) 10

(H) 1

(J) 0

Don't be nervous! It's important to get a good night's sleep before your test.

Properties

Directions: Read each problem. Find the correct answer. Fill in the circle.

1. **How many thousands are in 5,708?**

   Ⓐ 8

   Ⓑ 0

   Ⓒ 7

   Ⓓ 5

2. **How can you write 8,225 in expanded notation?**

   Ⓕ 8,000 + 200 + 5

   Ⓖ 800 + 20 + 5

   Ⓗ 8,000 + 200 + 20 + 5

   Ⓙ 8,200 + 200 + 25

3. **Which group of numbers has three odd numbers?**

   Ⓐ 8, 12, 15, 17, 20, 26, 30

   Ⓑ 7, 10, 12, 13, 19, 22, 36

   Ⓒ 2, 5, 8, 14, 18, 28, 32, 40

   Ⓓ 16, 27, 28, 29, 30, 34, 38

4. **Which number below has a 9 in the hundreds place?**

   Ⓕ 5,967

   Ⓖ 5,798

   Ⓗ 9,654

   Ⓙ 5,679

5. **Which of these numbers has a 1 in the tens place and a 7 in the ones place?**

   Ⓐ 710

   Ⓑ 701

   Ⓒ 517

   Ⓓ 471

6. **How many thousands are in 2,398?**

   Ⓕ 8

   Ⓖ 9

   Ⓗ 3

   Ⓙ 2

7. **Which group of numbers has no even numbers?**

   Ⓐ 3, 4, 7, 19, 26, 29, 31

   Ⓑ 2, 5, 12, 13, 23, 27, 33

   Ⓒ 1, 3, 5, 8, 11, 13, 15

   Ⓓ 1, 5, 9, 17, 19, 21, 25

8. **How may tens are in 4,670?**

   Ⓕ 0

   Ⓖ 6

   Ⓗ 7

   Ⓙ 4

Name _____ Date _____

Properties

Directions: Read each problem. Find the correct answer. Fill in the circle.

1. How can you write 50,468 in expanded notation?

Ⓐ 5,000 + 400 + 60 + 8

Ⓑ 50,000 + 400 + 68

Ⓒ 50,000 + 1,000 + 400 + 60 + 8

Ⓓ 50,000 + 400 + 60 + 8

2. 5 hundreds and 7 thousands equals _____.

Ⓕ 5,700

Ⓖ 7,050

Ⓗ 570

Ⓙ 7,500

3. What is another name for 339?

Ⓐ 3 thousands, 3 hundreds, and 9 tens

Ⓑ 3 hundreds, 3 tens, and 9 ones

Ⓒ 3 hundreds and 39 tens

Ⓓ 9 hundreds, 3 tens, and 3 hundreds

4. How can you write 33,429 in expanded notation?

Ⓕ 3,000 + 400 + 20 + 9

Ⓖ 3,000 + 300 + 400 + 29

Ⓗ 30,000 + 3,000 + 400 + 20 + 9

Ⓙ 33,000 + 420 + 9

5. What is another name for 7 hundreds, 2 tens, and 0 ones?

Ⓐ 702

Ⓑ 7,200

Ⓒ 720

Ⓓ 712

Read the questions carefully.
Try to think of an answer before you look at the choices.

Properties

Directions: Read each problem. Find the correct answer. Fill in the circle.

Example

Which of these is 479 rounded to the nearest hundred?

(A) 400

(B) 470

(C) 500

(D) 580

Answer: C

---

1. Which of these is closest in value to 190?

(A) 186

(B) 192

(C) 179

(D) 199

2. Which of these numbers shows 342 rounded to the nearest hundred?

(F) 340

(G) 400

(H) 440

(J) 300

3. Round these numbers to the nearest hundred: 575, 612, 499, 633, 590, 680. How many of them will be 600?

(A) 6

(B) 5

(C) 4

(D) 3

4. Which of these is 288 rounded to the nearest hundred?

(F) 200

(G) 300

(H) 280

(J) 380

5. Which number sentence would you use to estimate 97 × 9 to the nearest hundred?

(A) 90 × 5

(B) 100 × 5

(C) 90 × 10

(D) 100 × 10

6. Which of these is closest in value to 580?

(F) 592

(G) 578

(H) 583

(J) 569

Properties

MATH
146

Directions: Read each problem. Find the correct answer. Fill in the circle.

1. **Which of these numbers shows 6,402 rounded to the nearest thousand?**

   (A) 6,000

   (B) 6,500

   (C) 6,400

   (D) 7,000

2. **Round these numbers to the nearest hundred: 180, 144, 129, 157, 162, 120, 171. How many of them will be 200?**

   (F) 4

   (G) 3

   (H) 5

   (J) 0

3. **Which of these is closest in value to 4?**

   (A) 4.4

   (B) 3.6

   (C) 4.2

   (D) 3.9

4. **Round these numbers to the nearest hundred: 501, 568, 476, 621, 589, 459. How many of them will be 500?**

   (F) 2

   (G) 3

   (H) 5

   (J) 0

5. **Round 644 and 289 to the nearest hundred and add them together.**

   (A) 800

   (B) 900

   (C) 700

   (D) 1,000

6. **Which of these is 856 rounded to the nearest hundred?**

   (F) 850

   (G) 900

   (H) 800

   (J) 1,000

7. **Which of these is closest in value to 2?**

   (A) 1.2

   (B) 2.2

   (C) 1.1

   (D) 2.1

8. **Round 471 and 319 to the nearest hundred and add them together.**

   (F) 800

   (G) 900

   (H) 700

   (J) 600

Sample Test 7: Concepts

Directions: Read and work each problem. Find the correct answer. Fill in the circle.

Example

A squirrel had 15 acorns. He lost 7 of them. How can you find the number of acorns left?

- (A) add
- (B) subtract
- (C) multiply
- (D) divide

Answer: (B)

---

1. You are number 12 in a line of 20 people. How many people are behind you?

- (A) 9
- (B) 7
- (C) 8
- (D) 6

2. What is another name for 8 hundreds, 4 tens, and 3 ones?

- (F) 8,430
- (G) 843
- (H) 834
- (J) 8,043

3. Which number is greater than 754?

- (A) 759
- (B) 749
- (C) 745
- (D) 744

4. The picture below shows the number of cars parked in a lot. Which answer is the same number as is shown in the picture?

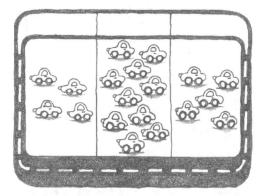

- (F) 100 + 40 + 5
- (G) 1 + 4 + 5
- (H) 400 + 100 + 5
- (J) 4 + 10 + 5

5. The number 644 is less than _____.

- (A) 643
- (B) 654
- (C) 640
- (D) 634

6. How many tens are in 2,674?

- (F) 2
- (G) 6
- (H) 4
- (J) 7

GO

Name _____ Date _____

Sample Test 7: Concepts

Directions: Read and work each problem. Find the correct answer. Fill in the circle.

7. Which number is represented by the chart?

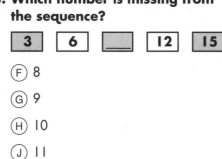

Hundreds	Tens	Ones
ⅠⅠⅠⅠⅠⅠ	ⅠⅠⅠⅠ ⅠⅠⅠⅠⅠ	ⅠⅠⅠⅠ

- (A) 964
- (B) 469
- (C) 696
- (D) 694

8. Which number is missing from the sequence?

| 3 | 6 | ___ | 12 | 15 |

- (F) 8
- (G) 9
- (H) 10
- (J) 11

9. Paul and Vesta used a computer to solve a problem. Which of these is the same as the number on the screen?

- (A) three thousand one hundred eighty
- (B) three hundred eighty
- (C) three thousand one hundred eight
- (D) three thousand eighteen

10. Round 3,322 to the nearest thousand.

- (F) 4,000
- (G) 3,300
- (H) 3,000
- (J) 4,300

11. From the figures below, you know that

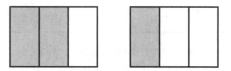

- (A) $\frac{1}{3}$ is greater than $\frac{2}{3}$.
- (B) $\frac{1}{2}$ is greater than $\frac{2}{3}$.
- (C) $\frac{2}{3}$ is greater than $\frac{1}{2}$.
- (D) $\frac{2}{3}$ is greater than $\frac{1}{3}$.

12. Count by fives. Which number comes after 25 and before 35?

- (F) 50
- (G) 20
- (H) 30
- (J) 40

13. Which of these fractions is the largest?

- (A) $\frac{2}{3}$
- (B) $\frac{1}{2}$
- (C) $\frac{1}{4}$
- (D) $\frac{2}{5}$

Sample Test 7: Concepts

Directions: Read and work each problem. Find the correct answer. Fill in the circle.

14. Which number is an even number and can be divided evenly by 7?

- (F) 26
- (G) 35
- (H) 14
- (J) 60

15. Which number sentence shows how to find the total number of butterflies?

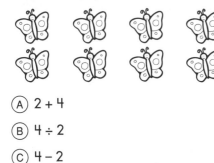

- (A) 2 + 4
- (B) 4 ÷ 2
- (C) 4 − 2
- (D) 2 × 4

16. 55 − □ = 23
29 + □ = 61
Which number completes both number sentences?

- (F) 23
- (G) 30
- (H) 32
- (J) 33

17. Which of these is closest in value to 2,000?

- (A) 1,979
- (B) 1,997
- (C) 2,004
- (D) 2,010

18. Which of these is 587 rounded to the nearest hundred?

- (F) 580
- (G) 500
- (H) 690
- (J) 600

19. Round these numbers to the nearest hundred: 179, 225, 212, 141, 255, 149. How many of them will be 200?

- (A) 3
- (B) 4
- (C) 5
- (D) 6

20. $\frac{1}{3} = \frac{\square}{6}$
What does the □ equal?

- (F) 2
- (G) 5
- (H) 4
- (J) 6

Sample Test 7: Concepts

Directions: Read and work each problem. Find the correct answer. Fill in the circle.

21. What is another name for 621?

Ⓐ 6 hundreds, 1 ten, and 2 ones

Ⓑ 6 hundreds, 2 tens, and 1 one

Ⓒ 6 thousands, 2 tens, and 1 one

Ⓓ 2 hundreds, 6 tens, and 1 one

22. Count by tens. Which number comes after 90 and before 110?

Ⓕ 95

Ⓖ 100

Ⓗ 105

Ⓙ 120

23. Which number is missing from the sequence?

50		60	65	70

Ⓐ 45

Ⓑ 55

Ⓒ 59

Ⓓ 75

24. Which equation describes this problem: Logan uses a $10 bill to buy a book for $6.95. How much change does he get back?

Ⓕ $6.95 × □ = $10.00

Ⓖ $10.00 + $6.95 = □

Ⓗ $10.00 − □ = $6.95

Ⓙ $10.00 − $6.95 = □

25. Which number makes this number sentence true?
$8 \times \square = 72$

Ⓐ 15

Ⓑ 12

Ⓒ 9

Ⓓ 8

26. 55 □ 7 = 48
Which operation sign belongs in the box?

Ⓕ +

Ⓖ −

Ⓗ ×

Ⓙ ÷

27. What is another name for 314?

Ⓐ 3 hundreds, 14 tens

Ⓑ 3 hundreds, 4 tens, 1 one

Ⓒ 3 thousands, 1 ten, 4 ones

Ⓓ 3 hundreds, 1 ten, 4 ones

Addition

Directions: Mark the space for the correct answer to each addition problem. Choose "None of these" if the answer is not given.

Example

39 + 21 =

Ⓐ 59

Ⓑ 61

Ⓒ 65

Ⓓ None of these

Answer: D

1. 37
    +11

Ⓐ 44

Ⓑ 46

Ⓒ 48

Ⓓ None of these

2. 299
    + 54

Ⓕ 335

Ⓖ 353

Ⓗ 355

Ⓙ None of these

3. 12 + 29 + 6 =

Ⓐ 45

Ⓑ 49

Ⓒ 47

Ⓓ None of these

4. 33 + 33 + 33 =

Ⓕ 90

Ⓖ 96

Ⓗ 98

Ⓙ None of these

5. 519
    + 56

Ⓐ 575

Ⓑ 557

Ⓒ 577

Ⓓ None of these

6. 6.97
    +1.62

Ⓕ 8.95

Ⓖ 8.59

Ⓗ 8.49

Ⓙ None of these

7. 270
    955
    +116

Ⓐ 1,343

Ⓑ 1,431

Ⓒ 1,340

Ⓓ None of these

8. 12 + 17 + 25 =

Ⓕ 45

Ⓖ 55

Ⓗ 54

Ⓙ None of these

The answer in an addition problem is always larger than the numbers being added.

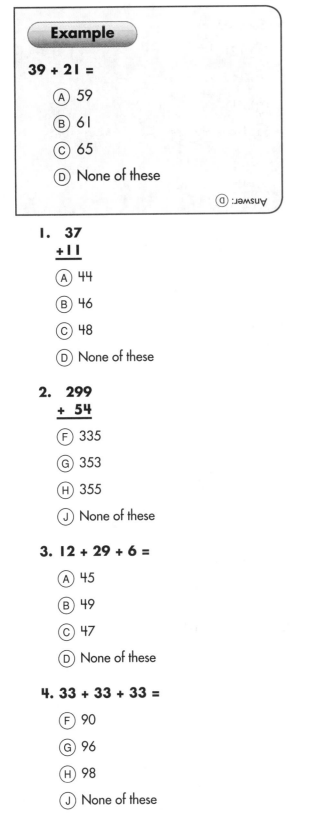

Addition

Directions: Mark the space for the correct answer to each addition problem. Choose "None of these" if the answer is not given.

1. $\frac{1}{5} + \frac{1}{6} =$

   (A) $\frac{5}{12}$

   (B) $\frac{1}{12}$

   (C) $\frac{5}{6}$

   (D) None of these

2. $39 + 21 + 44 =$

   (F) 102

   (G) 105

   (H) 109

   (J) None of these

3. 370
   +119

   (A) 449

   (B) 489

   (C) 499

   (D) None of these

4. 7,562
   + 177

   (F) 7,779

   (G) 7,379

   (H) 7,739

   (J) None of these

5. $1.55 + $2.39 =

   (A) $3.99

   (B) $3.49

   (C) $3.93

   (D) None of these

6. $56 + 65 =$

   (F) 121

   (G) 112

   (H) 211

   (J) None of these

7. 555
   +545

   (A) 1,100

   (B) 1,001

   (C) 1,010

   (D) None of these

8. 4.56
   +4.67

   (F) 9.13

   (G) 9.23

   (H) 9.32

   (J) None of these

9. $20.09 + $1.18 =

   (A) $21.17

   (B) $20.27

   (C) $21.27

   (D) None of these

10. $11 + 12 + 13 =$

   (F) 32

   (G) 34

   (H) 35

   (J) None of these

Addition

Directions: Mark the space for the correct answer to each addition problem. Choose "None of these" if the answer is not given.

1.   444
     602
    +138

   (A) 1,284

   (B) 1,048

   (C) 1,184

   (D) None of these

2. $\frac{1}{8} + \frac{6}{8} =$

   (F) $\frac{5}{8}$

   (G) $\frac{6}{8}$

   (H) $\frac{7}{8}$

   (J) None of these

3.   5.98
    +2.11

   (A) 8.09

   (B) 8.19

   (C) 7.19

   (D) None of these

4. $9.82 + $1.40 =

   (F) $11.23

   (G) $10.22

   (H) $11.02

   (J) None of these

5.   188
    + 62

   (A) 205

   (B) 250

   (C) 260

   (D) None of these

6. 65 + 86 + 22 =

   (F) 163

   (G) 173

   (H) 175

   (J) None of these

7. $\frac{1}{3} + \frac{1}{3} =$

   (A) $\frac{2}{3}$

   (B) $\frac{1}{3}$

   (C) $\frac{2}{6}$

   (D) None of these

8. 1.2 + 8.6 + 3.2 =

   (F) 13

   (G) 13.2

   (H) 12.9

   (J) None of these

Addition

154

Directions: Mark the space for the correct answer to each addition problem. Choose "None of these" if the answer is not given.

1. 18 + 24 + 7 =

(A) 59

(B) 58

(C) 48

(D) None of these

2. $62.14 + $25.01 =

(F) $87.14

(G) $86.15

(H) $87.15

(J) None of these

3. 6 + 6 + 6 + 6 =

(A) 22

(B) 24

(C) 30

(D) None of these

4. 6.67 + 5.12 =

(F) 11.79

(G) 11.97

(H) 12.79

(J) None of these

5. 6,947
+ 202

(A) 7,149

(B) 7,148

(C) 7,159

(D) None of these

6. $\frac{1}{2} + \frac{1}{2} =$

(F) $\frac{1}{4}$

(G) 1

(H) $\frac{1}{2}$

(J) None of these

7. 4.2
+7.5

(A) 11.9

(B) 11.07

(C) 12.7

(D) None of these

8. 29 + 48 =

(F) 67

(G) 76

(H) 77

(J) None of these

Addition

Directions: Mark the space for the correct answer to each addition problem. Choose "None of these" if the answer is not given.

1. $\frac{2}{8} + \frac{5}{8} =$
    - (A) $\frac{7}{16}$
    - (B) $\frac{7}{8}$
    - (C) $\frac{8}{8}$
    - (D) None of these

2. $\begin{array}{r} 345 \\ +129 \\ \hline \end{array}$
    - (F) 464
    - (G) 574
    - (H) 475
    - (J) None of these

3. $2.8 + 4.3 + 3.0 =$
    - (A) 10
    - (B) 9.8
    - (C) 10.2
    - (D) None of these

4. $\begin{array}{r} \$2.99 \\ +\$1.99 \\ \hline \end{array}$
    - (F) $3.98
    - (G) $4.98
    - (H) $4.99
    - (J) None of these

5. $82 + 12 =$
    - (A) 94
    - (B) 96
    - (C) 92
    - (D) None of these

6. $\begin{array}{r} 201 \\ 844 \\ +653 \\ \hline \end{array}$
    - (F) 1,689
    - (G) 1,698
    - (H) 1,697
    - (J) None of these

7. $\$12.56 + \$2.34 =$
    - (A) $14.00
    - (B) $13.90
    - (C) $14.90
    - (D) None of these

8. $\frac{2}{5} + \frac{1}{5} =$
    - (F) $\frac{4}{5}$
    - (G) $\frac{3}{10}$
    - (H) $\frac{3}{5}$
    - (J) None of these

Subtraction

Directions: Mark the space for the correct answer to each subtraction problem. Choose "None of these" if the correct answer is not given.

Example

23
– 5

- (A) 16
- (B) 18
- (C) 20
- (D) None of these

Answer: (B)

1. 62
– 17

- (A) 44
- (B) 46
- (C) 45
- (D) None of these

2. 200
– 80

- (F) 30
- (G) 10
- (H) 20
- (J) None of these

3. 55 – 5 – 9 =

- (A) 40
- (B) 41
- (C) 42
- (D) None of these

4. 444 – 44 – 4 =

- (F) 440
- (G) 436
- (H) 410
- (J) None of these

5. 4.17
– 0.50

- (A) 3.67
- (B) 3.77
- (C) 3.66
- (D) None of these

6. 7.17
– 1.62

- (F) 5.45
- (G) 5.57
- (H) 5.55
- (J) None of these

7. 9,550
– 7,010

- (A) 2,450
- (B) 2,540
- (C) 2,550
- (D) None of these

8. 22 – 17

- (F) 3
- (G) 4
- (H) 5
- (J) None of these

When you are not sure about an answer to a subtraction problem, check it by adding.

Subtraction

Directions: Mark the space for the correct answer to each subtraction problem. Choose "None of these" if the correct answer is not given.

1. $\frac{7}{9} - \frac{4}{9} =$

   (A) $\frac{3}{9}$

   (B) $\frac{3}{18}$

   (C) $\frac{11}{9}$

   (D) None of these

2. $0.39 - $0.12 =

   (F) $0.20

   (G) $0.26

   (H) $0.29

   (J) None of these

3.   373
  −369

   (A) 2

   (B) 3

   (C) 4

   (D) None of these

4.   8,661
  − 120

   (F) 8,441

   (G) 8,451

   (H) 8,541

   (J) None of these

5. $6.52 − $2.36 =

   (A) $4.14

   (B) $4.15

   (C) $4.16

   (D) None of these

6. 98 − 89 =

   (F) 7

   (G) 9

   (H) 8

   (J) None of these

7.   500
  − 50

   (A) 400

   (B) 550

   (C) 50

   (D) None of these

8.   4.56
  −4.52

   (F) 0.04

   (G) 0.40

   (H) 9.38

   (J) None of these

9. $10.01 − $0.92 =

   (A) $9.90

   (B) $9.01

   (C) $9.09

   (D) None of these

10. $\frac{5}{6} - \frac{4}{6} =$

   (F) $\frac{9}{6}$

   (G) $\frac{1}{12}$

   (H) $\frac{1}{6}$

   (J) None of these

Name _____ Date _____

Subtraction

Directions: Mark the space for the correct answer to each subtraction problem. Choose "None of these" if the correct answer is not given.

1. $7.89 – $1.44

- (A) $5.46
- (B) $6.54
- (C) $6.45
- (D) None of these

2. $\frac{3}{6} - \frac{1}{6} =$

- (F) $\frac{2}{6}$
- (G) $\frac{3}{6}$
- (H) $\frac{2}{12}$
- (J) None of these

3. 8.22
     – 3.14

- (A) 5.06
- (B) 4.08
- (C) 5.16
- (D) None of these

4. 845 – 76 – 55 =

- (F) 714
- (G) 741
- (H) 724
- (J) None of these

5. 9.00
     – 5.27

- (A) 3.75
- (B) 3.73
- (C) 3.37
- (D) None of these

6. 95
     – 57

- (F) 38
- (G) 28
- (H) 32
- (J) None of these

7. $12.12
     – $ 7.45

- (A) $4.67
- (B) $4.76
- (C) $5.33
- (D) $4.93

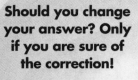

Should you change your answer? Only if you are sure of the correction!

Chapter 8: Computation

Subtraction

Directions: Mark the space for the correct answer to each subtraction problem. Choose "None of these" if the correct answer is not given.

1. 58 – 12 – 10 =
   - (A) 38
   - (B) 36
   - (C) 28
   - (D) None of these

2. 29
   – 14
   - (F) 17
   - (G) 16
   - (H) 15
   - (J) None of these

3. $3.04
   – $1.92
   - (A) $1.21
   - (B) $2.22
   - (C) $1.12
   - (D) None of these

4. $\frac{6}{8} - \frac{2}{8} =$
   - (F) $\frac{4}{16}$
   - (G) 4
   - (H) $\frac{4}{8}$
   - (J) None of these

5. 2,450
   – 649
   - (A) 1,801
   - (B) 1,800
   - (C) 1,799
   - (D) None of these

6. $25 – $6.50 =
   - (F) $19.50
   - (G) $18.50
   - (H) $18.05
   - (J) None of these

7. 68 – 39 =
   - (A) 29
   - (B) 39
   - (C) 27
   - (D) None of these

8. 1.66
   – 0.58
   - (F) 1.16
   - (G) 1.06
   - (H) 1.08
   - (J) None of these

MATH
160

Subtraction

Directions: Mark the space for the correct answer to each subtraction problem. Choose "None of these" if the correct answer is not given.

1. $14.91
   -$ 6.15

   (A) $8.75

   (B) $8.66

   (C) $7.76

   (D) None of these

2. 32 – 22 – 8 =

   (F) 6

   (G) 4

   (H) 2

   (J) None of these

3. 1,422
   - 351

   (A) 1,071

   (B) 1,070

   (C) 1,710

   (D) None of these

4. $\frac{4}{5} - \frac{2}{5} =$

   (F) $\frac{2}{10}$

   (G) $\frac{4}{5}$

   (H) $\frac{2}{5}$

   (J) None of these

5. $30 – $15.50 =

   (A) $14.00

   (B) $14.50

   (C) $15.50

   (D) None of these

6. 12,000 – 6,000 =

   (F) 600

   (G) 60,000

   (H) 6,000

   (J) None of these

7. 54
   - 19

   (A) 45

   (B) 42

   (C) 36

   (D) None of these

8. $0.98 – $0.14 =

   (F) $1.12

   (G) $0.84

   (H) $0.88

   (J) None of these

Multiplication and Division

Directions: Mark the space for the correct answer to each problem. Choose "None of these" if the correct answer is not given.

Examples

A.   3
    × 4

Ⓐ 7

Ⓑ 10

Ⓒ 12

Ⓓ None of these

Answer: Ⓒ

B. 10 ÷ 2 =

Ⓕ 2

Ⓖ 4

Ⓗ 5

Ⓙ None of these

Answer: Ⓗ

---

1. 4 × 0 =

Ⓐ 0

Ⓑ 4

Ⓒ 8

Ⓓ None of these

2. 6)‾13

Ⓕ 2

Ⓖ 2 R1

Ⓗ 2 R2

Ⓙ None of these

3.   7
    ×10

Ⓐ 77

Ⓑ 17

Ⓒ 70

Ⓓ None of these

4. 6)‾36

Ⓕ 7

Ⓖ 8

Ⓗ 9

Ⓙ None of these

5. 17 ÷ 8 =

Ⓐ 2 R2

Ⓑ 2 R3

Ⓒ 2 R4

Ⓓ None of these

6. 4)‾200

Ⓕ 80

Ⓖ 50

Ⓗ 40

Ⓙ None of these

7.   210
    ×   5

Ⓐ 1,050

Ⓑ 1,500

Ⓒ 1,005

Ⓓ None of these

8. 10 × ☐ = 20

Ⓕ 1

Ⓖ 0

Ⓗ 2

Ⓙ None of these

Pay close attention to the operation sign in each equation.

Multiplication and Division

Directions: Mark the space for the correct answer to each problem. Choose "None of these" if the correct answer is not given.

1. 201
    × 3
    - (A) 600
    - (B) 601
    - (C) 603
    - (D) None of these

2. 9 ÷ 9 =
    - (F) 1
    - (G) 2
    - (H) 3
    - (J) None of these

3. 4 × 11 =
    - (A) 40
    - (B) 44
    - (C) 48
    - (D) None of these

4. 0)12
    - (F) 12
    - (G) 12 R1
    - (H) 0
    - (J) None of these

5. 12
    ×11
    - (A) 132
    - (B) 120
    - (C) 144
    - (D) None of these

6. 6)68
    - (F) 11 R2
    - (G) 11 R3
    - (H) 11 R4
    - (J) None of these

7. 32 ÷ 4 =
    - (A) 6
    - (B) 2
    - (C) 4
    - (D) None of these

8. 4)42
    - (F) 10
    - (G) 10 R1
    - (H) 11
    - (J) None of these

9. 300
    × 5
    - (A) 1,000
    - (B) 1,500
    - (C) 5,000
    - (D) None of these

10. 12 × □ = 48
    - (F) 2
    - (G) 3
    - (H) 4
    - (J) None of these

Multiplication and Division

Directions: Mark the space for the correct answer to each problem. Choose "None of these" if the correct answer is not given.

1. 40 ÷ 2 =

(A) 10

(B) 4

(C) 25

(D) None of these

2. 77 ÷ 7 =

(F) 7

(G) 14

(H) 11

(J) None of these

3. 544
× 2

(A) 1,808

(B) 1,088

(C) 1,800

(D) None of these

4. 9)83

(F) 9 R1

(G) 9 R2

(H) 9

(J) None of these

5. 12
× 7

(A) 48

(B) 96

(C) 82

(D) None of these

6. 1)42

(F) 1

(G) 42

(H) 21

(J) None of these

7. 604
× 5

(A) 3,020

(B) 320

(C) 3,002

(D) None of these

8. 5 × □ = 45

(F) 9

(G) 7

(H) 8

(J) None of these

9. 9 × 7 =

(A) 36

(B) 63

(C) 72

(D) None of these

10. 6)42

(F) 6

(G) 7

(H) 8

(J) None of these

Multiplication and Division

Directions: Mark the space for the correct answer to each problem. Choose "None of these" if the correct answer is not given.

1. $7 \times \square = 28$
   - (A) 3
   - (B) 4
   - (C) 6
   - (D) None of these

2. 2,283
   $\times$ 3
   - (F) 6,849
   - (G) 6,489
   - (H) 5,899
   - (J) None of these

3. $7\overline{)42}$
   - (A) 5
   - (B) 6
   - (C) 7
   - (D) None of these

4. $150 \div 10 =$
   - (F) 10
   - (G) 15
   - (H) 5
   - (J) None of these

5. 39
   $\times$ 8
   - (A) 212
   - (B) 302
   - (C) 312
   - (D) None of these

6. 822
   $\times$ 4
   - (F) 3,286
   - (G) 3,822
   - (H) 3,282
   - (J) None of these

7. $4\overline{)48}$
   - (A) 8
   - (B) 6
   - (C) 12
   - (D) None of these

8. $\square \div 9 = 9$
   - (F) 9
   - (G) 72
   - (H) 81
   - (J) None of these

9. $6 \times \square = 6$
   - (A) 0
   - (B) 1
   - (C) 6
   - (D) None of these

10. $45 \div 9 =$
   - (F) 9
   - (G) 6
   - (H) 5
   - (J) None of these

Relating Multiplication and Division

Directions: Read and work each problem. Find the correct answer. Fill in the circle.

Example

64 ÷ 8 = □
8 × □ = 64

(A) 9
(B) 8
(C) 12
(D) 56

Answer: B

1. 32 ÷ 16 = 2
16 × □ = 32

(A) 32
(B) 16
(C) 2
(D) 8

2. 25 ÷ 5 = □
5 × □ = 25

(F) 5
(G) 25
(H) 50
(J) 10

3. 81 ÷ 9 = □
9 × □ = 81

(A) 3
(B) 81
(C) 12
(D) 9

4. 144 ÷ 12 = □
12 × □ = 144

(F) 48
(G) 14
(H) 24
(J) 12

5. 56 ÷ 14 = □
14 × □ = 56

(A) 6
(B) 4
(C) 8
(D) 9

6. 143 ÷ 11 = □
11 × □ = 143

(F) 12
(G) 11
(H) 14
(J) 13

7. 36 ÷ 4 = □
4 × □ = 36

(A) 6
(B) 3
(C) 11
(D) 9

Relating Multiplication and Division

Directions: Read and work each problem. Find the correct answer. Fill in the circle.

1. $3 \times \square = 27$
   $27 \div \square = 3$
   - (A) 3
   - (B) 27
   - (C) 9
   - (D) 8

2. $7 \times \square = 56$
   $56 \div 7 = \square$
   - (F) 8
   - (G) 9
   - (H) 14
   - (J) 28

3. $13 \times 3 = \square$
   $\square \div 3 = 13$
   - (A) 16
   - (B) 26
   - (C) 39
   - (D) 52

4. $11 \times \square = 121$
   $121 \div \square = 11$
   - (F) 10
   - (G) 11
   - (H) 12
   - (J) 13

5. $36 \div 6 = \square$
   $6 \times \square = 36$
   - (A) 36
   - (B) 60
   - (C) 42
   - (D) 6

6. $48 \div 12 = \square$
   $12 \times \square = 48$
   - (F) 4
   - (G) 6
   - (H) 8
   - (J) 12

7. $99 \div 9 = \square$
   $9 \times \square = 99$
   - (A) 9
   - (B) 12
   - (C) 10
   - (D) 11

8. $54 \div 2 = \square$
   $2 \times \square = 54$
   - (F) 24
   - (G) 13
   - (H) 27
   - (J) 26

Relating Multiplication and Division

Directions: Read and work each problem. Find the correct answer. Fill in the circle.

1. 8 × □ = 16
   16 ÷ □ = 8

   (A) 2
   (B) 3
   (C) 4
   (D) 6

2. 56 ÷ 8 = □
   8 × □ = 56

   (F) 9
   (G) 7
   (H) 6
   (J) 8

3. 30 ÷ 5 = □
   5 × □ = 30

   (A) 5
   (B) 8
   (C) 6
   (D) 7

4. 5 × □ = 55
   55 ÷ □ = 5

   (F) 5
   (G) 10
   (H) 11
   (J) 21

5. 5 × □ = 60
   60 ÷ 5 = □

   (A) 12
   (B) 10
   (C) 16
   (D) 8

6. 49 ÷ 7 = □
   7 × □ = 49

   (F) 11
   (G) 9
   (H) 8
   (J) 7

Always read the directions carefully!

Relating Multiplication and Division

MATH
(168)

Directions: Read and work each problem. Find the correct answer. Fill in the circle.

1. 72 ÷ 8 = ☐
    8 × ☐ = 72
- (A) 8
- (B) 9
- (C) 7
- (D) 12

2. 11 × ☐ = 110
    110 ÷ ☐ = 11
- (F) 10
- (G) 11
- (H) 12
- (J) 100

3. 24 ÷ 3 = ☐
    3 × ☐ = 24
- (A) 3
- (B) 4
- (C) 8
- (D) 12

4. 54 ÷ 6 = ☐
    6 × ☐ = 54
- (F) 9
- (G) 6
- (H) 13
- (J) 8

5. 9 × ☐ = 81
    81 ÷ 9 = ☐
- (A) 3
- (B) 11
- (C) 9
- (D) 7

6. 12 × ☐ = 60
    60 ÷ ☐ = 12
- (F) 6
- (G) 5
- (H) 10
- (J) 8

7. 64 ÷ 4 = ☐
    4 × ☐ = 64
- (A) 16
- (B) 4
- (C) 8
- (D) 14

8. 80 ÷ 10 = ☐
    10 × ☐ = 80
- (F) 11
- (G) 8
- (H) 10
- (J) 18

Name _____ Date _____

Estimating

Directions: Read and work each problem. Find the correct answer. Fill in the circle.

Example

Suppose you wanted to estimate how to find 73 + 48 to the nearest ten. Which of these would you use?

- Ⓐ 100 + 40
- Ⓑ 100 + 50
- Ⓒ 70 + 50
- Ⓓ 70 + 40

Answer: Ⓒ

1. Which of these is the best way to estimate the answer to this problem?
   28 – 19 =☐
   - Ⓐ 30 – 10 = ☐
   - Ⓑ 20 – 10 = ☐
   - Ⓒ 30 – 20 = ☐
   - Ⓓ 10 – 10 = ☐

2. Which number sentence would you use to estimate 97 + 9 to the nearest ten?
   - Ⓕ 90 + 5
   - Ⓖ 100 + 10
   - Ⓗ 90 + 10
   - Ⓙ 100 + 5

3. Use estimation to find which of these is closest to 100.
   - Ⓐ 39 + 58
   - Ⓑ 49 + 40
   - Ⓒ 59 + 57
   - Ⓓ 91 + 18

4. A group of people brought their pets to a street fair: 33 people brought dogs, 18 people brought cats, and 11 people brought other kinds of pets. Which of these estimates is closest to the total number of people who brought pets?
   - Ⓕ 50
   - Ⓖ 60
   - Ⓗ 70
   - Ⓙ 80

5. Michael was at a card convention. At the first booth, he bought 8 cards. He bought 6 cards at the next booth and 13 at the last booth. Which of these estimates is closest to the number of cards Michael bought?
   - Ⓐ 10
   - Ⓑ 15
   - Ⓒ 20
   - Ⓓ 30

6. Use estimation to find which of these number sentences is closest to 60.
   - Ⓕ 32 + 26
   - Ⓖ 45 + 26
   - Ⓗ 78 + 15
   - Ⓙ 28 + 42

Chapter 8: Computation

Ready to Test • Third Grade

Estimating

MATH
170

Directions: Read and work each problem. Find the correct answer. Fill in the circle.

1. How would you estimate 73 × 48 to the nearest ten?

Ⓐ 100 × 40

Ⓑ 100 × 50

Ⓒ 70 × 40

Ⓓ 70 × 50

2. Emerson Elementary makes $297 on the first day of the book fair. They make $333 on the second day. On the last day of the fair, they make $502. Which of these estimates is closest to the total amount of money the school made?

Ⓕ $1,000

Ⓖ $1,100

Ⓗ $1,200

Ⓙ $1,300

3. Which of these is the best way to estimate the answer to this problem?
42 + 38 = ☐

Ⓐ 40 + 30 = ☐

Ⓑ 30 + 30 = ☐

Ⓒ 40 + 40 = ☐

Ⓓ 50 + 30 = ☐

4. Which of these is the best way to estimate the answer to this problem?
1,456 – 1,220 = ☐

Ⓕ 1,000 – 1,000 = ☐

Ⓖ 1,500 – 1,000 = ☐

Ⓗ 1,500 – 1,200 = ☐

Ⓙ 2,000 – 1,200 = ☐

5. How would you estimate 679 + 348 to the nearest hundred?

Ⓐ 700 + 400

Ⓑ 700 + 300

Ⓒ 680 + 350

Ⓓ 600 + 300

If two answer choices seem like they could be correct, compare them for differences. Then, reread the question to find your best answer.

Estimating

Directions: Read and work each problem. Find the correct answer. Fill in the circle.

1. Which of these is the best way to estimate the answer to this problem?
$18 \times 26 = \Box$

   (A) $20 \times 30 = \Box$

   (B) $10 \times 30 = \Box$

   (C) $20 \times 20 = \Box$

   (D) $10 \times 20 = \Box$

2. Which number sentence would you use to estimate $96 \div 12$ to the nearest ten?

   (F) $100 \div 10$

   (G) $100 \div 20$

   (H) $90 \div 20$

   (J) $90 \div 10$

3. Olivia collected leaf specimens for a science project. She collected 8 on Tuesday, 14 on Wednesday, and 27 during the weekend. Which of these estimates is closest to the total number of leaves Olivia collected?

   (A) 40

   (B) 50

   (C) 60

   (D) 70

4. How would you estimate $542 - 229$ to the nearest hundred?

   (F) $500 - 300$

   (G) $500 - 200$

   (H) $600 - 300$

   (J) $600 - 200$

5. There are 589 jelly beans in a jar. Sonya guessed there were 537. Aiden guessed there were 602. Molly guessed there were 577. Vijay guessed there were 591. Estimate to the nearest ten to see whose guess was closest.

   (A) Sonya

   (B) Aiden

   (C) Molly

   (D) Vijay

6. Use estimation to find which of these number sentences is closest to 80.

   (F) $29 + 54$

   (G) $39 + 60$

   (H) $18 + 47$

   (J) $32 + 62$

7. Which of these is the best way to estimate the answer to this problem?
$87 - 29 = \Box$

   (A) $100 - 30$

   (B) $80 - 20$

   (C) $90 - 20$

   (D) $90 - 30$

Estimating

Directions: Read and work each problem. Find the correct answer. Fill in the circle.

1. Which number sentence would you use to estimate 42 + 16 to the nearest ten?

Ⓐ 40 + 10

Ⓑ 40 + 20

Ⓒ 50 + 10

Ⓓ 50 + 20

2. Katrina has 55 stamps in her collection, Owen has 72, and Abbas has 19. Which of these estimates is closest to the total number of stamps the three friends have?

Ⓕ 130

Ⓖ 140

Ⓗ 150

Ⓙ 160

3. Which number sentence would you use to estimate 68 – 55 to the nearest 10?

Ⓐ 60 – 50

Ⓑ 60 – 60

Ⓒ 70 – 50

Ⓓ 70 – 60

4. The Samson family has been observing birds in their backyard. Yesterday, they saw 13 chickadees, 27 finches, 4 cardinals, and 8 robins. Which of these estimates is closest to the total number of birds the family observed?

Ⓕ 50

Ⓖ 40

Ⓗ 70

Ⓙ 30

5. Which of these is the best way to estimate the answer to this problem?
$47 \div 9 = \square$

Ⓐ $40 \div 10 = \square$

Ⓑ $40 \div 0 = \square$

Ⓒ $50 \div 0 = \square$

Ⓓ $50 \div 10 = \square$

6. Use estimation to find which of these number sentences is closest to 200.

Ⓕ 27×11

Ⓖ $199 + 28$

Ⓗ $379 - 68$

Ⓙ 18×7

Sample Test 8: Computation

Directions: Mark the space for the correct answer to each problem. Choose "None of these" if the correct answer is not given.

Examples

A. 555
    + 99

Ⓐ 655

Ⓑ 456

Ⓒ 654

Ⓓ None of these

Answer: C

B. 78 − 39 =

Ⓕ 117

Ⓖ 39

Ⓗ 59

Ⓙ None of these

Answer: G

---

1. 444
    − 66

Ⓐ 550

Ⓑ 510

Ⓒ 378

Ⓓ None of these

2. $\frac{4}{5} - \frac{1}{5} =$

Ⓕ $\frac{3}{5}$

Ⓖ $\frac{2}{5}$

Ⓗ $\frac{5}{5}$

Ⓙ None of these

3. $\frac{3}{4} - \frac{1}{4} =$

Ⓐ $\frac{2}{4}$

Ⓑ $\frac{1}{4}$

Ⓒ $\frac{4}{4}$

Ⓓ None of these

4. 65 + 61 + 7 =

Ⓕ 122

Ⓖ 123

Ⓗ 133

Ⓙ None of these

5. 9,000
    −5,010

Ⓐ 3,900

Ⓑ 3,909

Ⓒ 3,990

Ⓓ None of these

6. 6.98
    − 1.55

Ⓕ 5.45

Ⓖ 5.57

Ⓗ 5.55

Ⓙ None of these

7. 519
    + 56

Ⓐ 543

Ⓑ 545

Ⓒ 533

Ⓓ None of these

8. 35 − 19 =

Ⓕ 16

Ⓖ 17

Ⓗ 19

Ⓙ None of these

9. 10 + 31 + 8 =

Ⓐ 50

Ⓑ 49

Ⓒ 47

Ⓓ None of these

GO

Sample Test 8: Computation

Directions: Mark the space for the correct answer to each problem. Choose "None of these" if the correct answer is not given.

10. $0.37 + $6.19 =

- (F) $6.56
- (G) $6.50
- (H) $6.47
- (J) None of these

11. 300
   ×   5

- (A) 1,000
- (B) 1,500
- (C) 5,000
- (D) None of these

12. 12 × □ = 48

- (F) 2
- (G) 3
- (H) 4
- (J) None of these

13. 222
   + 11

- (A) 232
- (B) 231
- (C) 233
- (D) None of these

14. 3,904
   +   154

- (F) 4,185
- (G) 4,158
- (H) 4,058
- (J) None of these

15. $\frac{3}{4} - \frac{2}{4}$ =

- (A) $\frac{2}{4}$
- (B) $\frac{1}{4}$
- (C) $\frac{4}{4}$
- (D) None of these

16. 1)$\overline{50}$

- (F) 50
- (G) 5
- (H) 0
- (J) None of these

17. 93 × 6 =

- (A) 99
- (B) 548
- (C) 558
- (D) None of these

18. 7)$\overline{77}$

- (F) 10 R1
- (G) 11
- (H) 11 R1
- (J) None of these

19. 4,009
   −   27

- (A) 4,036
- (B) 3,982
- (C) 3,992
- (D) None of these

20. 5.91
   − 2.39

- (F) 8.30
- (G) 3.52
- (H) 3.62
- (J) None of these

21. $1\frac{4}{5} - \frac{1}{5}$ =

- (A) 2
- (B) $1\frac{1}{5}$
- (C) $1\frac{3}{5}$
- (D) None of these

Name _____ Date _____

Sample Test 8: Computation

Directions: Mark the space for the correct answer to each problem. Choose "None of these" if the correct answer is not given.

22. $2.00 – $1.17 =

- (F) $0.38
- (G) $0.88
- (H) $3.17
- (J) None of these

23.
$$6,788$$
$$+\ \ 999$$

- (A) 5,789
- (B) 7,777
- (C) 7,787
- (D) None of these

24.
$$578$$
$$+\ 34$$

- (F) 612
- (G) 613
- (H) 544
- (J) None of these

25. $\frac{3}{8} - \frac{1}{8}$

- (A) $\frac{4}{8}$
- (B) $\frac{5}{8}$
- (C) $\frac{2}{8}$
- (D) None of these

26. $7\overline{)3,577}$

- (F) 500
- (G) 210 R1
- (H) 511
- (J) None of these

27.
$$\$5.67$$
$$+\$1.23$$

- (A) $6.90
- (B) $4.54
- (C) $4.44
- (D) None of these

28.
$$6.02$$
$$+3.91$$

- (F) 2.11
- (G) 9.93
- (H) 9.91
- (J) None of these

29.
$$84$$
$$\times 11$$

- (A) 920
- (B) 924
- (C) 824
- (D) None of these

30. $10\overline{)100}$

- (F) 11
- (G) 10
- (H) 1
- (J) None of these

31. $\frac{1}{3} + \frac{2}{3} + 1 =$

- (A) $3\frac{1}{3}$
- (B) 2
- (C) 3
- (D) None of these

32. $12.00 – $3.91 =

- (F) $15.91
- (G) $8.01
- (H) $8.09
- (J) None of these

33. $99 \div 9 =$

- (A) 9
- (B) 12
- (C) 10
- (D) None of these

GO

Sample Test 8: Computation

Directions: Mark the space for the correct answer to each problem. Choose "None of these" if the correct answer is not given.

34. $24 \div 2 = \square$
$2 \times \square = 24$

(F) 6

(G) 12

(H) 8

(J) None of these

35. $6 \times 7 = \square$
$\square \div 7 = 6$

(A) 43

(B) 35

(C) 49

(D) None of these

36. $4 \times \square = 16$
$16 \div 4 = \square$

(F) 4

(G) 8

(H) 12

(J) None of these

37. $55 \div 11 = \square$
$11 \times \square = 55$

(A) 11

(B) 5

(C) 10

(D) None of these

38. Which of these is the best way to estimate the answer to this problem?
$16 + 58 = \square$

(F) $20 + 50 = \square$

(G) $10 + 50 = \square$

(H) $20 + 60 = \square$

(J) None of these

39. Ty counted backyard bugs for a school project. He saw 12 spiders, 67 ants, 33 bees, and 19 butterflies. Which of these estimates is closest to the total number of bugs Ty counted?

(A) 100

(B) 120

(C) 130

(D) None of these

40. There were 260 people in the auditorium for the school play. Aisha guessed there were 269. Liza guessed there were 257. Oliver guessed there were 251. Yoshi guessed there were 272. Estimate to the nearest ten to see whose guess was closest.

(F) Aisha

(G) Liza

(H) Oliver

(J) None of these

41. Use estimation to find which of these number sentences is closest to 150.

(A) $69 + 82$

(B) $98 + 64$

(C) $32 + 127$

(D) None of these

STOP

Symmetry and Reflection

Directions: Read and work each problem. Find the correct answer. Fill in the circle.

1. Which of the figures below does not show a line of symmetry?

Ⓐ
Ⓑ
Ⓒ
Ⓓ

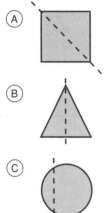

2. Which of these letters has a line of symmetry?

Ⓕ **Q**

Ⓖ **P**

Ⓗ **N**

Ⓙ **M**

3. Look at the letters below. Which one does not have a line of symmetry?

Ⓐ **G**

Ⓑ **T**

Ⓒ **O**

Ⓓ **X**

4. If you folded the figures below in half, which one would not have a line of symmetry?

Ⓕ
Ⓖ
Ⓗ
Ⓙ

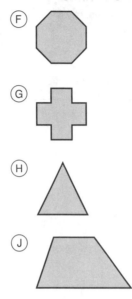

5. Which of these letters is not symmetrical?

Ⓐ **H**

Ⓑ **O**

Ⓒ **X**

Ⓓ **Z**

> Remember, if you fold the figure on the line of symmetry, the two halves match up perfectly!

Name _____ Date _____

Reflection and Rotation

Directions: For the drawings below, write *reflection* or *rotation* to describe how the figure was moved.

Reflection is one kind of symmetry. In reflection, a figure is flipped, creating a mirror image.

E∃

Rotation is another kind of symmetry. In rotation, a figure is rotated around a fixed point.

5ꙅ

1.

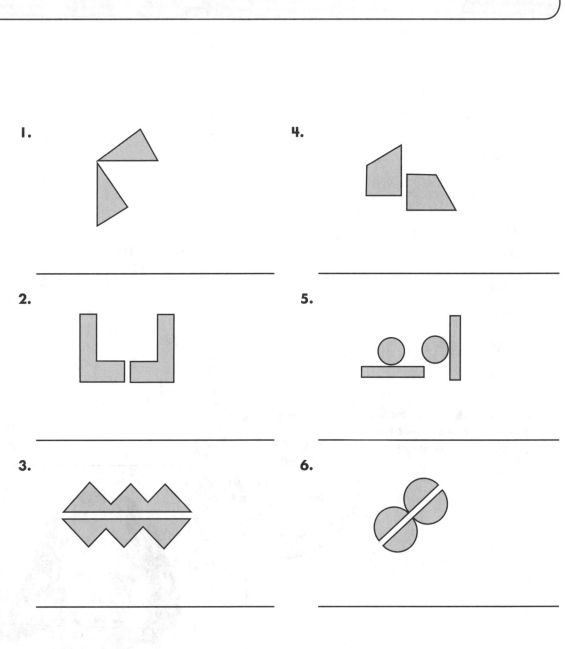

2.

_____

3.

_____

4.

_____

5.

_____

6.

_____

Shapes and Figures

Directions: Read each problem. Find the correct answer. Fill in the circle.

1. Look at the picture of the castle made with blocks. Which shape was used only one time?

- Ⓐ circle
- Ⓑ triangle
- Ⓒ rectangle
- Ⓓ square

2. Look at the shapes below. Which one is to the right of the largest circle?

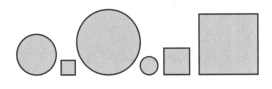

- Ⓕ the largest square
- Ⓖ the smallest circle
- Ⓗ the smallest square
- Ⓙ the medium-sized circle

3. This shape is called a

- Ⓐ pentagon.
- Ⓑ hexagon.
- Ⓒ octagon.
- Ⓓ triangle.

4. A four-sided figure could be a

- Ⓕ circle.
- Ⓖ triangle.
- Ⓗ square.
- Ⓙ pentagon.

> Pay close attention to any pictures, key words, and numbers in the problems. Some problems will be easier to solve if you use scrap paper.

Shapes and Figures

Directions: Read each problem. Find the correct answer. Fill in the circle.

1. Which of the following is a four-sided figure?

(A) a hexagon

(B) an oval

(C) an octagon

(D) a quadrilateral

2. A polygon with three sides and three vertices is a

(F) square.

(G) triangle.

(H) rectangular prism.

(J) octagon.

3. This shape is called a

(A) circle.

(B) sphere.

(C) pentagon.

(D) pyramid.

4. Which of these figures is not the same shape and size as the others?

(F)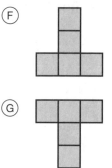

(G)

(H)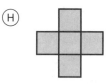

(J)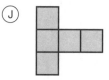

5. This shape is called a

(A) square

(B) trapezoid

(C) pentagon

(D) rectangle

Name _____   Date _____

Shapes and Figures

Directions: Read each problem. Find the correct answer. Fill in the circle.

1. **A polygon that has 6 sides and 6 angles is a(n) _____.**

   Ⓐ pentagon

   Ⓑ hexagon

   Ⓒ octagon

   Ⓓ trapezoid

2. **Which polygon has more sides than a hexagon?**

   Ⓕ pentagon

   Ⓖ triangle

   Ⓗ octagon

   Ⓙ square

3. **How many sides does a quadrilateral have?**

   Ⓐ 3 sides

   Ⓑ 4 sides

   Ⓒ 5 sides

   Ⓓ 6 sides

4. **A polygon that has only one pair of parallel sides is a _____.**

   Ⓕ parallelogram

   Ⓖ quadrilateral

   Ⓗ hexagon

   Ⓙ trapezoid

5. **How is a square different from a rectangle?**

   Ⓐ A square has 4 equal sides.

   Ⓑ A square has 2 equal sides.

   Ⓒ A square has right angles.

   Ⓓ A square has parallel sides.

6. **If you were to draw a figure with no sides or angles, what would it look like?**

   Ⓕ

   Ⓖ

   Ⓗ

   Ⓙ

Are you going to guess at an answer?
Try to use hints from questions you know to answer questions you don't know.

Ready to Test • Third Grade

Shapes and Figures

Directions: Read and work each problem. Find the correct answer. Fill in the circle.

1. Which polygon has fewer sides than a square?

(A) a pentagon

(B) a triangle

(C) an octagon

(D) a square

2. Which statement is not true?

(F) A circle has no vertices.

(G) A hexagon has more sides than a pentagon.

(H) A pyramid is a 3-D shape.

(J) A trapezoid has no parallel sides.

3. Look at the shapes below. Which one is to the left of the trapezoid?

(A) pentagon

(B) octagon

(C) circle

(D) rectangle

4. Which figure shows parallel lines?

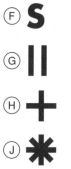

(F) S

(G) ||

(H) +

(J) ✳

5. A polygon that has 5 sides and 5 angles is a _____.

(A) square

(B) hexagon

(C) octagon

(D) pentagon

6. Which statement is true?

(F) A triangle never has more than 3 sides.

(G) A square has only 2 parallel sides.

(H) An octagon has 6 sides.

(J) All 3 sides must be of equal length in a triangle.

3-D Shapes

Directions: Read and work each problem. Find the correct answer. Fill in the circle.

1. A basketball is shaped like a

(A) pyramid.

(B) circle.

(C) sphere.

(D) rectangle.

2. Which of these objects is shaped like a cube?

(F)

(G)

(H)

(J)

3. What three solid objects have been used to make this object?

(A) sphere, cylinder, rectangular prism

(B) cube, cylinder, pyramid

(C) pyramid, cylinder, square

(D) cone, cylinder, cube

4. Which of the following is not a 3-D figure?

(F) a sphere

(G) a cone

(H) a rectangular prism

(J) a trapezoid

5. A can of soup is shaped like a

(A) pyramid.

(B) sphere.

(C) cylinder.

(D) trapezoid.

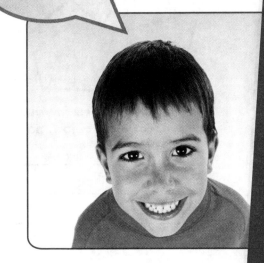

Don't forget to to keep an eye on how much time you have left.

Name _____   Date _____

3-D Shapes

Directions: Draw a line to match each 3-D shape with a 2-D shape. Some shapes will have more than one line.

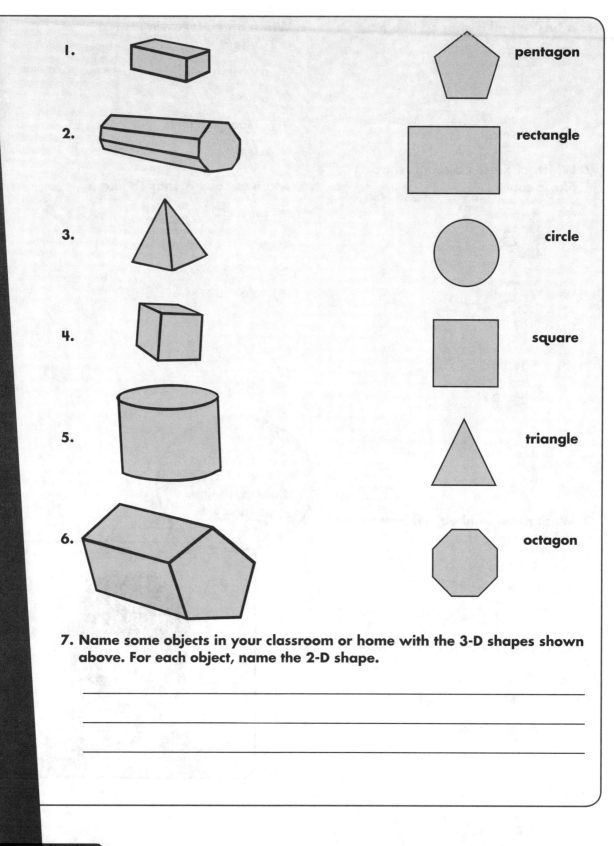

1.

2.

3.

4.

5.

6.

pentagon

rectangle

circle

square

triangle

octagon

7. **Name some objects in your classroom or home with the 3-D shapes shown above. For each object, name the 2-D shape.**

_____

_____

_____

3-D Shapes

Directions: Follow the instructions for each item below.

1. Draw a real-life object in the shape of a cone.

2. Draw a real-life object in the shape of a cube.

3. Draw a real-life object in the shape of a sphere.

4. Draw a real-life object in the shape of a cylinder.

5. Draw a real-life object in the shape of a rectangular prism.

Area and Perimeter

Directions: Read and work each problem. Find the correct answer. Fill in the circle.

Example

Look at the picture of the tile floor. What is the area of the gray tiles?

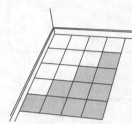

(A) 9 square units

(B) 5 square units

(C) 11 square units

(D) 10 square units

Answer: (D)

1. Look at the shaded area in this picture. If each square is an inch, what is the area of the shaded part?

(A) 289 square inches

(B) 150 square inches

(C) 19 square inches

(D) 17 square inches

2. What is the perimeter of the polygon?

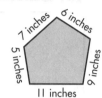

(F) 38 inches

(G) 26 inches

(H) 28 inches

(J) Not enough information

3. If the perimeter of this figure is 88 inches, the missing side is

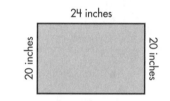

(A) 12 inches long.

(B) 20 inches long.

(C) 24 inches long.

(D) Not enough information

4. Look at the figure. What is its area and perimeter?

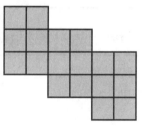

(F) The area is 18 square units, and the perimeter is 22 units.

(G) The area is 22 square units, and the perimeter is 14 units.

(H) The area is 16 square units, and the perimeter is 14 units.

(J) Not enough information

Area and Perimeter

Directions: Read and work each problem. Find the correct answer. Fill in the circle.

1. Look at the shaded area in this square. If each square is an inch, what is the area of the shaded part?

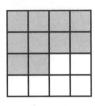

- Ⓐ 16 square inches
- Ⓑ 15 square inches
- Ⓒ 12 square inches
- Ⓓ 10 square inches

2. Elana wants to put a fence around her flower garden. How many feet of fencing will she need?

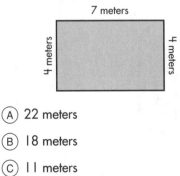

- Ⓕ 22 ft.
- Ⓖ 50 ft.
- Ⓗ 62 ft.
- Ⓙ 33 ft.

3. What is the perimeter of the rectangle?

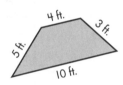

7 meters
4 meters
4 meters

- Ⓐ 22 meters
- Ⓑ 18 meters
- Ⓒ 11 meters
- Ⓓ 3 meters

4. What is the area of the shaded region?

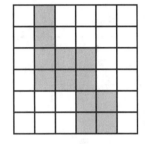

- Ⓕ 36 square units
- Ⓖ 20 square units
- Ⓗ 12 square units
- Ⓙ 24 square units

5. What is the perimeter of an octagon whose sides measure 6 inches each?

- Ⓐ 6 inches
- Ⓑ 24 inches
- Ⓒ 36 inches
- Ⓓ 48 inches

6. Kylie is sewing a doll quilt. It is 14 inches long and 10 inches wide. How much ribbon will she need to go around the edge of the quilt?

- Ⓕ 14 inches
- Ⓖ 28 inches
- Ⓗ 48 inches
- Ⓙ 54 inches

Using Coordinates

Directions: On the grid below, plot the points that are listed at the bottom of this page. Label each point with its letter. Point **L**, the library, has been plotted for you at (4,5).

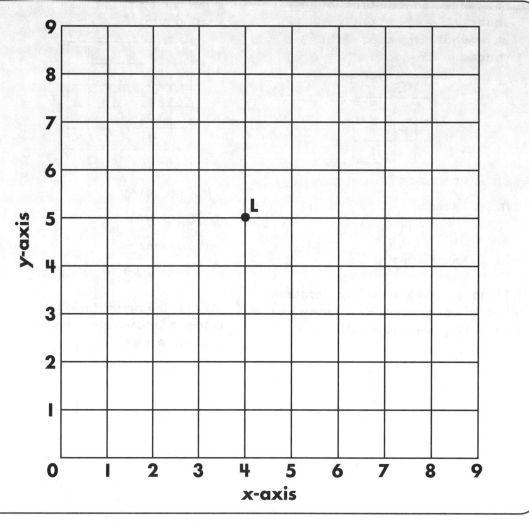

Point C (2, 7) coffee shop   **Point P (6, 3) park**
Point F (5, 6) fire station   **Point S (7, 5) school**
Point H (4, 2) hospital   **Point T (1, 0) train station**

> **Remember, the first number represents the horizontal axis (or x-axis). The second number represents the vertical axis (or y-axis).**

Using Coordinates

Directions: Use the grid to find the location of each of the points in the park listed below. Write the coordinates on the line.

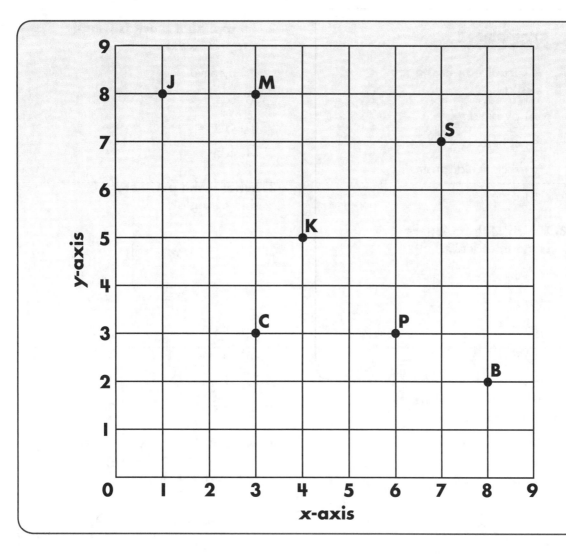

Point **S**, the swing set _____

Point **K**, the carousel _____

Point **P**, the pond _____

Point **B**, the batting cages _____

Point **J**, the jungle gym _____

Point **M**, the monkey bars _____

Point **C**, the climbing wall _____

Sample Test 9: Geometry

190

Directions: Read and work each problem. Find the correct answer. Fill in the circle.

Examples

A. A cereal box is shaped like a

- Ⓐ pyramid.
- Ⓑ sphere.
- Ⓒ rectangular prism.
- Ⓓ cone.

Answer: Ⓒ

B. Which of these letters is symmetrical?

- Ⓕ J
- Ⓖ M
- Ⓗ P
- Ⓙ B

Answer: Ⓖ

1. Which of these shapes is symmetrical?

Ⓐ

Ⓑ

Ⓒ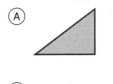

Ⓓ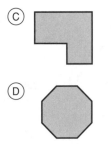

2. An alphabet block is usually shaped like a

- Ⓕ pyramid.
- Ⓖ cone.
- Ⓗ cylinder.
- Ⓙ cube.

3. What is the perimeter of this triangle?

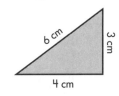

6 cm   3 cm   4 cm

- Ⓐ 13 cm
- Ⓑ 12 cm
- Ⓒ 17 cm
- Ⓓ 18 cm

4. Look at the shapes below. Which one is to the right of the smallest circle?

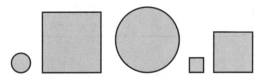

- Ⓕ the largest circle
- Ⓖ the medium-sized square
- Ⓗ the largest square
- Ⓙ the smallest square

GO

Sample Test 9: Geometry

Directions: Read and work each problem. Find the correct answer. Fill in the circle.

5. Which of these words contains a letter that does not have a line of symmetry?

(A) **ABOUT**

(B) **BALD**

(C) **CAVE**

(D) **MOTH**

6. Which word describes the movement of the figure below?

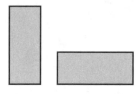

(F) rotation

(G) rectangle

(H) perimeter

(J) reflection

7. A rectangle measures 11 inches on one side and 8 on another. Which number sentence shows how you would find the rectangle's perimeter?

(A) $11 + 8 = \square$

(B) $11 \times 8 = \square$

(C) $11 + 11 + 8 + 8 = \square$

(D) $11 \times 11 \times 8 \times 8 = \square$

8. Mr. Selena is getting new carpeting in his living room. His living room measures 12 feet by 16 feet. He wants to know how much carpeting he'll need. Which number sentence shows how he could find out?

(F) $12 \times 16 = \square$

(G) $12 + 12 + 16 + 16 = \square$

(H) $16 \div 12 = \square$

(J) $12 + 16 = \square$

9. Which of the following is not a four-sided figure?

(A) a rectangle

(B) a parallelogram

(C) a quadrilateral

(D) a pentagon

10. Which 2-D shape matches the 3-D shape below?

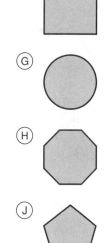

(F)

(G)

(H)

(J)

Measuring

Directions: Read and work each problem. Find the correct answer. Fill in the circle.

Example

Which of the following is the longest?

- Ⓐ 8 feet
- Ⓑ 3 yards
- Ⓒ 72 inches
- Ⓓ 1 yard 2 feet

Answer: (B)

---

1. How many inches long is the fish?

- Ⓐ 5 inches
- Ⓑ 6 inches
- Ⓒ 8 inches
- Ⓓ 12 inches

2. Look at the paper clip and the pencils. Which pencil is about 3 inches longer than the paper clip?

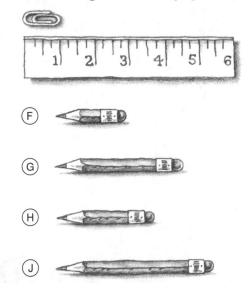

- Ⓕ
- Ⓖ
- Ⓗ
- Ⓙ

3. Angela wants to measure a piece of wood. Which of these should she use?

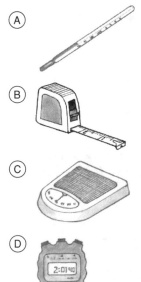

- Ⓐ
- Ⓑ
- Ⓒ
- Ⓓ

4. Which of the following is the longest?

- Ⓕ 1 foot
- Ⓖ 3 yards
- Ⓗ 18 inches
- Ⓙ 3 feet

Measuring

Directions: Read and work each problem. Find the correct answer. Fill in the circle.

1. Which of these statements is not true?

Ⓐ 1 yard = 39 inches

Ⓑ 1 foot = 12 inches

Ⓒ 1 pint = 2 cups

Ⓓ 6 feet = 72 inches

2. Which of the following is most likely to be measured in inches?

Ⓕ the width of a TV screen

Ⓖ the length of a football field

Ⓗ the distance to the library

Ⓙ the height of a skyscraper

3. How many inches long is the pencil?

Ⓐ 3 inches

Ⓑ 4 inches

Ⓒ 6 inches

Ⓓ 8 inches

4. Cooper wants to find the weight of a box of cereal. What unit of measurement will he probably find on the side of the box?

Ⓕ millimeters

Ⓖ pounds

Ⓗ hectoliters

Ⓙ ounces

5. If each of these nails were 1.5 centimeters long, how long would they be if you laid them end to end?

Ⓐ 10 centimeters

Ⓑ 11 centimeters

Ⓒ 12 centimeters

Ⓓ 13 centimeters

> When you're taking a test, read through the questions quickly and answer the easiest ones first. Then, you can use the rest of your time for the trickier ones!

Measuring

Directions: Read and work each problem. Find the correct answer. Fill in the circle.

1. **Which measurement is about right for a piece of chicken you might eat with dinner?**

   (A) 4 ounces

   (B) 14 ounces

   (C) 22 ounces

   (D) 1 pound

2. **Which statement is not true?**

   (F) The ounce is a unit for measuring weight.

   (G) The kilometer is a unit for measuring distance.

   (H) The second is a unit for measuring time.

   (J) The liter is a unit for measuring temperature.

3. **Which of these is the same as 10 millimeters?**

   (A) 1 meter

   (B) 1 kilometer

   (C) 1 centimeter

   (D) 1 decimeter

4. **Caroline has a book that is 12 inches long. If she laid three copies of this book end to end, they would measure _____.**

   (F) 2 feet

   (G) 12 feet

   (H) 1 yard

   (J) 3 yards

5. **Which of the following shows the correct order from smallest to largest?**

   (A) centimeter, millimeter, meter, kilometer

   (B) millimeter, centimeter, meter, kilometer

   (C) millimeter, centimeter, kilometer, meter

   (D) None of these

6. **Which of the following is most likely to be measured in millimeters?**

   (F) the length of a car

   (G) the length of a beetle

   (H) the height of a tree

   (J) the width of a room

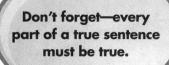

Don't forget—every part of a true sentence must be true.

Chapter 10: Measurement

Comparing Units of Length

Directions: Fill in the blanks with the equivalent measurement. Use the chart below to help you.

1 foot = 12 inches

1 yard = 3 feet

1 mile = 5,280 feet

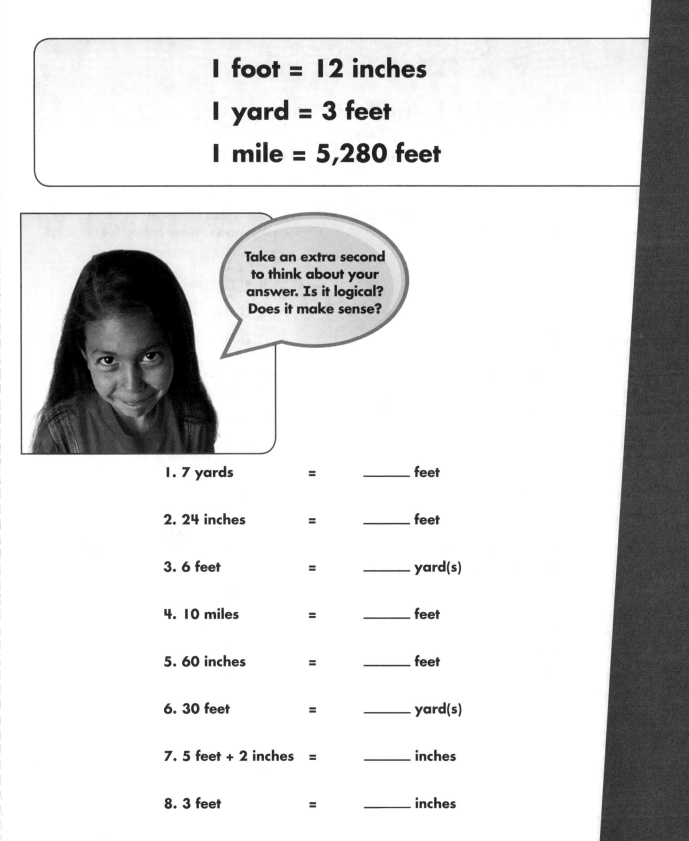

Take an extra second to think about your answer. Is it logical? Does it make sense?

1. 7 yards   =   _____ feet

2. 24 inches   =   _____ feet

3. 6 feet   =   _____ yard(s)

4. 10 miles   =   _____ feet

5. 60 inches   =   _____ feet

6. 30 feet   =   _____ yard(s)

7. 5 feet + 2 inches   =   _____ inches

8. 3 feet   =   _____ inches

Comparing Units of Length

Directions: Use the chart to help you answer the questions that follow. Fill in the circle.

1 foot = 12 inches
1 yard = 3 feet
1 mile = 5,280 feet

1. **Jess is 4 feet 2 inches tall. How tall is she in inches?**

   Ⓐ 42 inches

   Ⓑ 48 inches

   Ⓒ 50 inches

   Ⓓ 56 inches

2. **Zahara needs 2 yards of fabric to make a sundress. She has 8 feet of fabric. How much will be leftover?**

   Ⓕ 1 foot

   Ⓖ 2 feet

   Ⓗ 3 feet

   Ⓙ 0 feet

3. **Alex's backyard is 36 feet wide. How many yards wide is it?**

   Ⓐ 3 yards

   Ⓑ 18 yards

   Ⓒ 12 yards

   Ⓓ 6 yards

4. **Juan rides his bike 4 miles every afternoon. How many feet is this?**

   Ⓕ 21,120 feet

   Ⓖ 21,000 feet

   Ⓗ 21,200 feet

   Ⓙ 2,100 feet

5. **Mr. Kimmel's desk is 2 yards wide. How many inches is this?**

   Ⓐ 36 inches

   Ⓑ 48 inches

   Ⓒ 84 inches

   Ⓓ 72 inches

6. **Bailey's school is half a mile away from her house. How many feet away is it?**

   Ⓕ 3,000 feet

   Ⓖ 5,280 feet

   Ⓗ 2,460 feet

   Ⓙ 2,640 feet

Comparing Units of Length

Directions: The metric measuring system is based on multiples of 10. Below is a chart of metric length conversions. Use the chart to help you answer the questions.

> # 1 centimeter (cm) = 10 millimeters (mm)
> # 1 meter (m) = 100 centimeters (cm)
> # 1 kilometer (km) = 1,000 meters (m)

1. Ellie measured her tomato plant. It was 34 centimeters. How many millimeters is this?

   _____

2. Maya has a plastic case that is 4 centimeters long. She found a shell that is 34 millimeters long. Will it fit in her case?

   _____

3. Kifa jumped 3 meters. How many centimeters is this?

   _____

4. Jordan's desk is 1 meter by 1 meter. He would like to put his science project inside his desk. The project is on poster board that is 95 centimeters by 110 centimeters. Will it fit inside his desk without sticking out?

   _____

5. Amar's room measures 10 meters by 12 meters. How would you find the room's measurement in centimeters?

   _____

Comparing Units of Length

Directions: Fill in the blanks with the equivalent measurement. Use the chart below to help you.

> ## 1 centimeter (cm) = 10 millimeters (mm)
> ## 1 meter (m) = 100 centimeters (cm)
> ## 1 kilometer (km) = 1,000 meters (m)

1. 3 meters   =   _____ centimeters

2. 5000 meters   =   _____ kilometers

3. 23 centimeters   =   _____ millimeters

4. 168 centimeters   =   _____ meters
                                    + _____ centimeters

5. 33 kilometers   =   _____ meters

6. 8 centimeters
   + 8 millimeters   =   _____ millimeters

7. 1 meter   =   _____ millimeters

8. 12 kilometers
   + 62 meters   =   _____ meters

9. 52 millimeters   =   _____ centimeters
                                    + _____ meters

Time and Temperature

Directions: Read and work each problem. Find the correct answer. Fill in the circle.

Example

What time does the clock show?

(A) 9:45

(B) 10:15

(C) 10:45

(D) 11:00

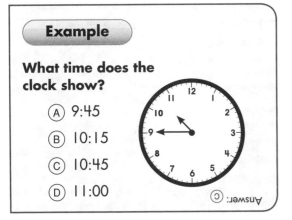

Answer: C

1. What is the temperature shown on the thermometer?

(A) 74°C

(B) 66°C

(C) 64°C

(D) 54°C

2. Pedro painted a picture of a house during art class. He worked for 40 minutes. The art class ended at 2:00. What time did Pedro start his picture?

(F) 1:30

(G) 1:20

(H) 1:10

(J) 1:40

3. Which statement is not true?

(A) 2 hours and 20 minutes = 90 minutes

(B) 4 hours = 240 minutes

(C) 2 minutes = 120 seconds

(D) 1 day = 24 hours

4. It takes a plane 4 hours to fly from Detroit to Los Angeles. This is the same as

(F) 180 minutes.

(G) 200 minutes.

(H) 240 minutes.

(J) 360 minutes.

5. How much did the average daily temperature change from February to March?

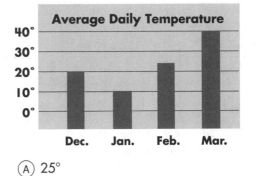

Average Daily Temperature

Dec. Jan. Feb. Mar.

(A) 25°

(B) 15°

(C) 10°

(D) 5°

6. A cake bakes for 1 hour and 10 minutes. This is the same as

(F) 60 minutes.

(G) 50 minutes.

(H) 70 minutes.

(J) 80 minutes.

Time and Temperature

Directions: Read and work each problem. Find the correct answer. Fill in the circle.

1. What time does the clock show?

Ⓐ 7:30

Ⓑ 7:20

Ⓒ 7:25

Ⓓ 7:35

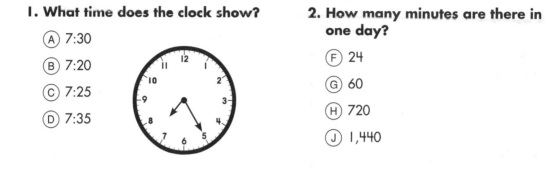

2. How many minutes are there in one day?

Ⓕ 24

Ⓖ 60

Ⓗ 720

Ⓙ 1,440

Directions: Use the January calendar page to answer questions 3–5.

January						
Sunday	Monday	Tuesday	Wednesday	Thursday	Friday	Saturday
					1	2 Concert
3 Family party for Chung	4	5 Chung's birthday	6	7	8	9 Maria's sledding party
10	11 Teacher Conference	12	13	14	15	16
17 Go to Grandma's for dinner	18	19	20 Science Fair	21	22	23
24	25	26 Field trip	27	28 Winter break	29 Winter break	30
31						

5. Chung's birthday is on January 5. If her book report is due on the following Tuesday, what date is it due?

Ⓐ January 19

Ⓑ January 11

Ⓒ January 18

Ⓓ January 12

3. What day of the week is Chung's birthday?

Ⓐ January 5

Ⓑ Tuesday

Ⓒ January 3

Ⓓ Saturday

4. What is the date of the last Sunday of the month?

Ⓕ January 31

Ⓖ January 24

Ⓗ January 30

Ⓙ January 17

Time and Temperature

Directions: Read and work each problem. Find the correct answer. Fill in the circle.

1. **Carrie loves to go skating. She went outside with her friends at 3:00. At 4:20, they came back inside. How long did they skate?**

   Ⓐ 60 minutes

   Ⓑ 50 minutes

   Ⓒ 70 minutes

   Ⓓ 80 minutes

2. **Which temperature would probably feel the most comfortable?**

   Ⓕ 20°F

   Ⓖ 35°F

   Ⓗ 90°F

   Ⓙ 70°F

3. **Look at the sign. If you just missed the 2:10 show, how many minutes will you need to wait for the next one?**

   AMAZING DOLPHIN SHOW!
   Daily at:
   1:15
   2:10
   3:05
   4:00
   4:50

   Ⓐ 50 minutes

   Ⓑ 45 minutes

   Ⓒ 60 minutes

   Ⓓ 55 minutes

Directions: Use the March calendar to answer questions 4 and 5.

			March			
Sunday	Monday	Tuesday	Wednesday	Thursday	Friday	Saturday
	1	2	3	4	5	6
7	8	9	10	11	12	13
14	15	16	17	18	19	20
21	22	23	24	25	26	27
28	29	30	31			

5. **On what day does March 11 fall?**

   Ⓐ Wednesday

   Ⓑ Thursday

   Ⓒ Friday

   Ⓓ Saturday

4. **What is the date of the last Wednesday of the month?**

   Ⓕ March 31

   Ⓖ March 30

   Ⓗ March 24

   Ⓙ March 29

Time and Temperature

Directions: Read and work each problem. Find the correct answer. Fill in the circle.

1. **Mr. Clemmons volunteers at Glenhaven Hospital. He has to be there at 4:00. It takes him 25 minutes to get to the hospital. What time should he leave his house?**

   Ⓐ 3:00

   Ⓑ 3:15

   Ⓒ 3:25

   Ⓓ 3:35

2. **A student won a juggling contest, keeping all three balls in the air for 7 minutes. If she started at 1:35, what time did she finish juggling?**

   Ⓕ 1:44

   Ⓖ 1:42

   Ⓗ 1:43

   Ⓙ 1:47

3. **What might the temperature be on a day when you are going sledding?**

   Ⓐ 65°F

   Ⓑ 80°F

   Ⓒ 58°F

   Ⓓ 25°F

4. **Ben and Annie are making dinner for their parents. It takes them 25 minutes to prepare everything, 40 minutes for the food to cook, and 10 minutes for them to set the table. How much time does it take them altogether?**

   Ⓕ 1 hour

   Ⓖ 1 hour and 10 minutes

   Ⓗ 1 hour and 15 minutes

   Ⓙ 1 hour and 35 minutes

5. **Look at the clock. Which clock below shows that 25 minutes have passed?**

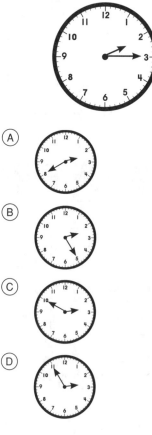

   Ⓐ

   Ⓑ

   Ⓒ

   Ⓓ

Time and Temperature

Directions: Read and work each problem. Find the correct answer. Fill in the circle.

1. It is 11:10. The bread Kim-Lee is making will be done in 40 minutes. Which clock shows what time the bread will be done?

Ⓐ

Ⓑ

Ⓒ

Ⓓ

2. It is 4:05. Caleb got home 15 minutes ago. Which clock shows what time he got home?

Ⓕ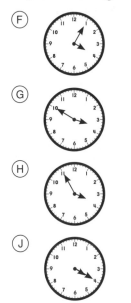

Ⓖ

Ⓗ

Ⓙ

3. Ms. Jacobi is due at work in half an hour. What time will it be then?

Ⓐ 7:45

Ⓑ 8:00

Ⓒ 8:15

Ⓓ 8:30

4. 480 seconds = _____ minutes

Ⓕ 60 minutes

Ⓖ 48 minutes

Ⓗ 6 minutes

Ⓙ 8 minutes

5. Look at the thermometers below. How much did the temperature rise during the day on Thursday?

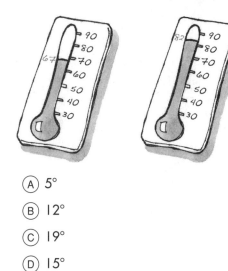

Ⓐ 5°

Ⓑ 12°

Ⓒ 19°

Ⓓ 15°

Name _____ Date _____

Money

Directions: Read and work each problem. Find the correct answer. Fill in the circle.

1. Josie has $7.00 in change. This is the same as _____.

   (A) 200 nickels

   (B) 60 dimes

   (C) 70 pennies

   (D) 28 quarters

2. Lilly rode her bike to the grocery store to buy some things for her mom. Here is the change she was given when she bought one of the items below with a $5 bill. Which item did she buy?

   (F)  Detergent 3.50

   (G) 2.50

   (H)  IceCream 2.95

   (J)  Coffee 3.65

3. Mr. Ruiz's bill at the diner was $11.22. He left a $2 tip, and he paid with a $20 bill. What was his change?

   (A) $6.98

   (B) $6.78

   (C) $5.98

   (D) $6.08

4. Max wants to buy a comic book that costs $0.95. Which combination of coins should he give the cashier?

   (F) 3 quarters and 2 dimes

   (G) 3 quarters and 2 nickels

   (H) 2 quarters and 4 dimes

   (J) 2 quarters, 3 dimes, and 2 nickels

5. Riga has a $5 bill and 3 quarters. Bryan has three $1 bills and 8 quarters. Tess has four $1 bills and 7 quarters. Who has the most money?

   (A) Riga

   (B) Bryan

   (C) Tess

   (D) Riga and Tess have the same amount.

Estimating Measurement

Directions: Read and work each problem. Find the correct answer. Fill in the circle.

1. Toby left his house for school at 7:33 A.M. He arrived at school at 7:50 A.M. About how many minutes did it take Toby to get to school?

Ⓐ 15 minutes

Ⓑ 25 minutes

Ⓒ 30 minutes

Ⓓ 10 minutes

2. Estimate the area of the shaded part of the figure. Choose the number that is most likely the area (in square units).

Ⓕ 3

Ⓖ 5

Ⓗ 9

Ⓙ 2

3. Which of these is most likely measured in feet?

Ⓐ the distance around a room

Ⓑ the weight of a large box

Ⓒ the distance to the moon

Ⓓ the amount of water in a pool

4. Lukas, Maria, and Diego decided to weigh themselves this morning. Lukas weighs 83 pounds, Maria weighs 79 pounds, and Diego weighs 88 pounds. About how much do they weigh altogether?

Ⓕ 250 pounds

Ⓖ 260 pounds

Ⓗ 240 pounds

Ⓙ 270 pounds

5. The zoo can't let animals outside unless the temperature is higher at least 50° by 10 A.M. The temperature at 10 on Monday was 42°. On Tuesday, the animals could go out. It was at least _____ degrees warmer on Tuesday.

Ⓐ 7

Ⓑ 8

Ⓒ 9

Ⓓ 10

Don't forget to read the directions carefully. You could miss out on some important information!

Name _____ Date _____

Sample Test 10: Measurement

Directions: Read and work each problem. Find the correct answer. Fill in the circle.

1. Rita left dance class at 3:30. She arrived home at 4:17. How long did it take Rita to get home?

(A) 1 hour and 17 minutes

(B) 47 minutes

(C) 37 minutes

(D) 13 minutes

2. Look at the calendar page. What is the date of the second Monday of the month?

March						
Sunday	Monday	Tuesday	Wednesday	Thursday	Friday	Saturday
	1	2	3	4	5	6
7	8	9	10	11	12	13
14	15	16	17	18	19	20
21	22	23	24	25	26	27
28	29	30	31			

(F) March 1

(G) March 7

(H) March 8

(J) March 2

3. Which sentence is not true?

(A) There are 3 yards in 1 foot.

(B) A kilometer is longer than a meter.

(C) There are more millimeters in a meter than centimeters.

(D) Kilometers and miles can both be used to measure distance.

4. The ferry to Rockport Island comes every 2 hours and 15 minutes. If the last ferry came at 1:15, what time will the next ferry come?

(F) 2:15

(G) 3:15

(H) 3:30

(J) 4:30

5. Which of these is most likely measured in millimeters?

(A) the weight of a leaf

(B) the distance across town

(C) the length of a bus

(D) the length of coin

6. How long is the paperclip?

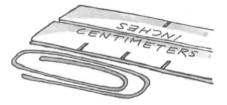

(F) 3 inches

(G) 5 inches

(H) 3 centimeters

(J) 2 centimeters

Sample Test 10: Measurement

Directions: Read and work each problem. Find the correct answer. Fill in the circle.

7. Maddy measured the length of the bathroom, which was 8 feet long. How many inches long is it?

(A) 16 inches

(B) 24 inches

(C) 96 inches

(D) 106 inches

8. In the morning, the temperature was 56°F. By noon, the temperature had risen 9°. How warm was it at noon?

(F) 60°F

(G) 64°F

(H) 65°F

(J) 70°F

9. Look at the clock below. What time was it 30 minutes ago?

(A) 6:15

(B) 6:30

(C) 6:20

(D) 7:20

10. Ava has 2 nickels, 3 quarters, and a penny. Iman has 4 dimes, 2 quarters, and 6 pennies. Zack has 3 nickels, 3 dimes, and 1 quarter. Who has the most money?

(F) Ava

(G) Iman

(H) Zack

(J) Ava and Iman have the same amount.

11. Will goes to his dentist appointment on April 4th. Afterwards, he makes his next appointment for a date 6 months away. When is his next appointment?

(A) in September

(B) in August

(C) in December

(D) in October

12. Charlotte left school at 2:45. She went to her grandma's house before going home. She arrived home at 3:35. How long could she have stayed at her grandma's house?

(F) 2 hours

(G) 1 hour

(H) 15 minutes

(J) 1 hour, 30 minutes

Probability

Example

A number cube is rolled. What is the probability of rolling a 4?

Ⓐ $\frac{1}{4}$

Ⓑ $\frac{1}{2}$

Ⓒ $\frac{1}{}$

Ⓓ $\frac{1}{6}$

Answer: Ⓓ

If you don't know the answer, it's okay to guess. But first, get rid of any answer choices you know are wrong.

Directions: Use the following information to answer the questions below. Fill in the circle.

Mackenzie put 3 yellow buttons, 6 red buttons, 2 blue buttons, and 1 green button in a bag. Li draws one button out of the bag each time.

1. What is the chance that Li will pull out a yellow button?

Ⓐ 3 out of 12

Ⓑ 4 out of 12

Ⓒ 1 out of 12

Ⓓ 6 out of 12

2. What is the chance that Li will pull out a blue button?

Ⓕ 1 out of 12

Ⓖ 4 out of 12

Ⓗ 5 out of 12

Ⓙ 2 out of 12

3. Which color is Li most likely to pull out?

Ⓐ yellow

Ⓑ blue

Ⓒ red

Ⓓ green

4. Which color is Li least likely to pull out?

Ⓕ yellow

Ⓖ blue

Ⓗ red

Ⓙ green

Probability

Directions: Use the following information to answer the questions below. Fill in the circle.

> In a grocery bag, there are 6 cans of tomato sauce, 4 cans of beans, and 9 cans of olives. All of the cans are the same size.

1. **If you reached into the bag without looking and picked out a can, what is the probability of picking a can of olives?**

   (A) $\frac{9}{19}$

   (B) $\frac{4}{19}$

   (C) $\frac{6}{19}$

   (D) $\frac{1}{19}$

2. **What is the probability of picking a can of beans?**

   (F) $\frac{1}{19}$

   (G) $\frac{4}{19}$

   (H) $\frac{6}{19}$

   (J) $\frac{9}{19}$

3. **What is the probability of picking a can of tomato sauce?**

   (A) $\frac{1}{19}$

   (B) $\frac{4}{19}$

   (C) $\frac{6}{19}$

   (D) $\frac{9}{19}$

4. **What type of can are you most likely to pull out?**

   (F) tomato sauce

   (G) beans

   (H) olives

   (J) Each can is equally likely to be chosen.

5. **What type of can are you least likely to pull out?**

   (A) tomato sauce

   (B) beans

   (C) olives

   (D) Each can is equally likely to be chosen.

Probability

Directions: Read each problem. Find the correct answer. Fill in the circle.

1. A number cube is rolled. What is the probability of rolling a 2?

(A) $\frac{1}{2}$

(B) $\frac{1}{4}$

(C) $\frac{1}{6}$

(D) $\frac{1}{8}$

2. A number cube is rolled. What is the probability of rolling a 2 or a 3?

(F) $\frac{1}{6}$

(G) $\frac{2}{6}$

(H) $\frac{3}{6}$

(J) $\frac{1}{2}$

Directions: Use the following information to answer questions 3–6.

Braden put 4 green marbles, 5 red marbles, 2 yellow marbles, and 1 purple marble in a jar. His sister closed her eyes and pulled out one at a time.

3. What is the chance that Braden's sister will pull out a yellow marble?

(A) 2 out of 12

(B) 2 out of 2

(C) 3 out of 8

(D) 2 out of 10

4. What is the chance that his sister will pull out a red marble?

(F) 5 out of 9

(G) 5 out of 5

(H) 5 out of 12

(J) 5 out of 11

5. What is the chance that she will pull out a purple marble?

(A) 1 out of 8

(B) 3 out of 12

(C) 1 out of 6

(D) 1 out of 12

6. Which color is Braden's sister least likely to pull out?

(F) green

(G) red

(H) purple

(J) yellow

Probability

Directions: Read each problem. Find the correct answer. Fill in the circle.

1. There are 8 boys and 12 girls in Ms. Phan's class. She draws a name out of a hat to decide who will be one of the captains of the kickball team. What are the chances that it will be a boy?

Ⓐ 1 out of 8

Ⓑ 1 out of 12

Ⓒ 8 out of 20

Ⓓ 8 out of 12

2. What are the chances that the team captain will be a girl?

Ⓕ 12 out of 20

Ⓖ 1 out of 12

Ⓗ 8 out of 20

Ⓙ 12 out of 12

3. The Romano family is trying to decide if they want to go to the beach, go camping, or go to the mountains for their vacation. They decide to write the ideas on slips of paper and choose one randomly. Which statement is true?

Ⓐ The camping trip is most likely to be chosen.

Ⓑ The beach trip is most likely to be chosen.

Ⓒ The mountain trip is most likely to be chosen.

Ⓓ Each vacation idea has an equal chance of being chosen.

4. The chances of the Romano family going camping are _____.

Ⓕ $\frac{3}{3}$

Ⓖ $\frac{1}{3}$

Ⓗ $\frac{2}{3}$

Ⓙ 0

5. Ryan flipped a coin. What are the chances that it will come up tails?

Ⓐ 0

Ⓑ 1 in 1

Ⓒ 1 in 2

Ⓓ 2 in 2

What if you can't find your answer among the choices? Try reading the question again. You might have misread it the first time.

Name _____   Date _____

Probability

Directions: Read each problem. Find the correct answer. Fill in the circle.

1. One letter is randomly chosen from the word *Mississippi*. What are the chances the letter will be an *s*?

- (A) 3 out of 11
- (B) 4 out of 11
- (C) 2 out of 11
- (D) 3 out of 12

2. One letter is randomly chosen from the word *terrific*. What are the chances the letter will be an *r*?

- (F) 4 out of 8
- (G) 2 out of 8
- (H) 1 out of 8
- (J) 1 out of 2

3. One letter is randomly chosen from the word *enjoyable*. What are the chances the letter will be a *y*?

- (A) 1 out of 9
- (B) 9 out of 9
- (C) 2 out of 8
- (D) 2 out of 9

4. One letter is randomly chosen from the word *irritating*. What are the chances the letter will be an *i*?

- (F) $\frac{2}{10}$
- (G) $\frac{3}{10}$
- (H) $\frac{3}{3}$
- (J) $\frac{10}{3}$

5. One letter is randomly chosen from the word *smooth*. What are the chances the letter will be an *o*?

- (A) $\frac{10}{2}$
- (B) $\frac{6}{6}$
- (C) $\frac{2}{6}$
- (D) $\frac{2}{10}$

6. One letter is randomly chosen from the word *child*. Which statement is not true?

- (F) The letters *c* and *h* are equally likely to be chosen.
- (G) The letters *d* and *h* are equally likely to be chosen.
- (H) The letter *i* is more likely to be chosen than *l*.
- (J) All the letters have an equal chance of being chosen.

7. One letter is randomly chosen from the word *strategic*. Which statement is not true?

- (A) The letters *g* and *c* are equally likely to be chosen.
- (B) The letters *s* and *a* are equally likely to be chosen.
- (C) The letter *t* is most likely to be chosen.
- (D) The letter *i* is least likely to be chosen.

Solving Word Problems

Directions: Read and work each problem. Find the correct answer. Fill in the circle.

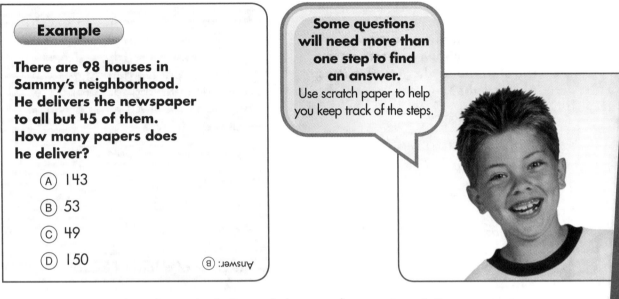

Example

There are 98 houses in Sammy's neighborhood. He delivers the newspaper to all but 45 of them. How many papers does he deliver?

- (A) 143
- (B) 53
- (C) 49
- (D) 150

Answer: (B)

Some questions will need more than one step to find an answer. Use scratch paper to help you keep track of the steps.

Directions: Use the information below to help you solve questions 1–3.

You have a bag of pretzels to share with your class. There are 25 students in your class. You want each student to get 7 pretzels.

1. What operation will you need to use to figure out how many pretzels you need?

- (A) addition
- (B) subtraction
- (C) multiplication
- (D) division

2. If two students are absent on the day you hand out the pretzels, how many will you have left over?

- (F) 10
- (G) 25
- (H) 12
- (J) 14

3. How many pretzels do you have in all?

- (A) 200
- (B) 175
- (C) 1,500
- (D) 145

4. A tsunami is a wave created by underwater earthquakes. Tsunamis can reach heights of 37 meters. How many centimeters tall is that?

- (F) 37,000 centimeters
- (G) 3,700 centimeters
- (H) 370 centimeters
- (J) 3.70 centimeters

Solving Word Problems

Directions: Read and work each problem. Find the correct answer. Fill in the circle.

1. **The music store had 757 customers last month and 662 customers this month. How many customers did the store have altogether in those two months?**

   (A) 1,409 customers

   (B) 1,419 customers

   (C) 1,429 customers

   (D) 1,439 customers

2. **Cameron has invited 5 girls and 3 boys to her birthday party. She plans to give each of her guests two balloons and keep one for herself. How many balloons will she need in all?**

   (F) 17 balloons

   (G) 9 balloons

   (H) 8 balloons

   (J) 18 balloons

3. **Amir has $3.00 to buy lunch. He chooses a sandwich that costs $1.50 and an orange that costs $0.45. How much money does he have left?**

   (A) $0.05

   (B) $1.05

   (C) $1.15

   (D) $1.60

4. **The trip from Homeville to Lincoln usually takes 25 minutes by car. While making the trip, a driver spent 12 minutes getting gas and 5 minutes waiting for a road crew. How long did it take the driver to make the trip?**

   (F) 32 minutes

   (G) 37 minutes

   (H) 48 minutes

   (J) 42 minutes

5. **The price of a loaf of bread was $1.29, but it increased by 8 cents. What is the new price of the bread?**

   (A) $1.21

   (B) $1.36

   (C) $1.37

   (D) $1.39

Don't forget to read the directions carefully.
You could miss an important word and answer incorrectly because of it!

Name _____   Date _____

Solving Word Problems

Directions: Read and work each problem. Find the correct answer. Fill in the circle.

1. **Isaiah wants to buy 3 books. Each book costs $3.95. How much will all three books cost?**

   Ⓐ $11.85

   Ⓑ $12.55

   Ⓒ $7.90

   Ⓓ $9.50

2. **Lola has 4 quarters and 2 dimes for bus fare. If the bus ride costs $0.75, how much money will she have left?**

   Ⓕ $0.25

   Ⓖ $0.35

   Ⓗ $0.45

   Ⓙ $0.50

3. **Jack is helping his mom make lemonade for a family picnic. To make a pitcher of lemonade, you need one can of frozen lemonade and 4 cups of water. How many cups of water will Jack need for 6 pitchers?**

   Ⓐ 16 cups

   Ⓑ 8 cups

   Ⓒ 32 cups

   Ⓓ 24 cups

4. **In the picture below, 1 book stands for 5 books. How many books does this picture stand for?**

   Ⓕ 25

   Ⓖ 45

   Ⓗ 40

   Ⓙ 30

5. **Riley's older sister is a lifeguard at the pool. She works for 6 hours and earns $54. Which number sentence shows how to find the amount of money Riley's sister earns in one hour?**

   Ⓐ $54 ÷ 6 = ☐

   Ⓑ $54 × 6 = ☐

   Ⓒ ☐ + 6 = $54

   Ⓓ $54 − ☐ = 6

6. **Seth has $5.50. If he buys 2 sodas for $0.75 each, how much money will he have left?**

   Ⓕ $4.50

   Ⓖ $0.75

   Ⓗ $4.00

   Ⓙ $3.00

Solving Word Problems

Directions: Read and work each problem. Find the correct answer. Fill in the circle.

1. **A worker at Command Software makes $720 a week. You want to figure out how much he makes an hour. What other piece of information do you need?**

   (A) the number of weeks he works each year

   (B) the number of vacation days he takes

   (C) how much money he makes each day

   (D) how many hours a day he works

2. **A single-scoop of frozen yogurt used to cost $1.39. The price has gone up 9 cents. How much does it cost now?**

   (F) $1.42

   (G) $1.48

   (H) $1.58

   (J) $1.30

Ahmad wants to buy baseball cards for his collection. At a sale, the cards are sold in packs. Look at the chart below. Use it to answer questions 3–6.

Number of Packs	Number of Cards
2	16
4	32
6	___
7	56

3. **If Ahmad bought three packs of baseball cards, how many cards would he have altogether?**

   (A) 18

   (B) 24

   (C) 32

   (D) 36

4. **What number sentence do you need to find the number of cards in each package?**

   (F) 2 × 16

   (G) 16 – 2

   (H) 16 ÷ 2

   (J) 56 – 7

5. **How many baseball cards are in each pack?**

   (A) 5

   (B) 6

   (C) 7

   (D) 8

6. **What is the missing number in the chart?**

   (F) 38

   (G) 42

   (H) 48

   (J) Not enough information

Treat each option as a true/false question. Choose the option that is the most true.

Chapter 11: Applications

Solving Word Problems

Directions: Read and work each problem. Find the correct answer. Fill in the circle.

1. What other equation belongs in the same fact family as 17 × 8 = 136?

(A) 13 × 8 = 104

(B) 136 ÷ 2 = 68

(C) 8 × 17 = 136

(D) 17 ÷ 8 = 25

2. In a desert garden, there are 6 rows of cactus plants. Each row has 5 plants. How many cactuses are there in the garden?

(F) 20

(G) 25

(H) 30

(J) 35

3. A doctor has her office open 5 days a week, 8 hours a day. If she sees 4 patients an hour, how many patients does she see in one day?

(A) 24

(B) 28

(C) 38

(D) 32

Directions: Read the information below. Use it to answer questions 4–6.

Abraham and his friends Luke and Esther bought a pizza. Abraham cut it into 6 equal pieces. He shared the pizza with his friends. Abraham had more than either Luke or Esther. Esther had more than Luke.

4. Who had the most pizza?

(F) Abraham

(G) Luke

(H) Esther

(J) Not enough information

5. If Esther had 2 pieces, how many pieces did Abraham have?

(A) 4

(B) 3

(C) 2

(D) 1

6. If the pizza cost $6.00, and the three friends split the cost equally, how much would they each pay?

(F) $1.00

(G) $2.00

(H) $3.00

(J) $4.00

Solving Word Problems

Directions: Read and work each problem. Find the correct answer. Fill in the circle.

1. DeShawn's sister has four coins. One is a nickel, and one is a dime. Which of these amounts might she have?

   Ⓐ 15 cents

   Ⓑ 20 cents

   Ⓒ 24 cents

   Ⓓ 30 cents

2. A total of 60 people brought their pets to the pet show. Half the people brought dogs, and 20 people brought cats. How many people brought other kinds of pets?

   Ⓕ 30 people

   Ⓖ 10 people

   Ⓗ 20 people

   Ⓙ 40 people

Use the menu to help you answer questions 3–5.

MENU

Hamburger $2.49
Cheeseburger $2.89
Taco $1.35
Chicken Sandwich $2.95
Milk $1.00
Lemonade $1.10

3. Choose the lunch item that costs the most.

   Ⓐ hamburger

   Ⓑ cheeseburger

   Ⓒ taco

   Ⓓ chicken sandwich

4. If you ordered a hamburger and lemonade, how much would they cost?

   Ⓕ $1.79

   Ⓖ $2.99

   Ⓗ $3.99

   Ⓙ $3.59

5. Choose the lunch that would cost the least.

   Ⓐ a taco and a milk

   Ⓑ a hamburger and a milk

   Ⓒ a chicken sandwich and a milk

   Ⓓ a taco and a lemonade

Solving Word Problems

Directions: Read and work each problem. Find the correct answer. Fill in the circle.

1. **Dominic has 5 grapes. How many grapes would he have if he adds 5 additional grapes each minute for 3 minutes?**

   (A) 15

   (B) 20

   (C) 25

   (D) None of these

2. **Which number sentence shows how to check the answer to question 1?**

   (F) $5 + 10 = 15$

   (G) $5 \times 3 + 5 = 20$

   (H) $5 \times 5 = 25$

   (J) None of these

3. **Taj carried 4 boxes of tiles into the kitchen. Each box held 12 tiles. How would you best determine the number of tiles he carried into the kitchen?**

   (A) multiply

   (B) subtract

   (C) divide

   (D) None of these

4. **Which number sentence shows the total number of tiles Taj carried into the kitchen?**

   (F) $4 \times 12 = 48$

   (G) $12 - 4 = 8$

   (H) $48 \div 8 = 6$

   (J) None of these

5. **The grocery store sells 5 cans of peas for $3.25. Which operation helps you find out how much each can cost?**

   (A) addition

   (B) subtraction

   (C) multiplication

   (D) division

6. **If Melanie buys 10 cans of peas and each can costs $0.65, how much does she pay?**

   (F) $6.50

   (G) $5.25

   (H) $6.25

   (J) $7.65

Solving Word Problems

Directions: Read and work each problem. Find the correct answer. Fill in the circle.

1. There are 762 CD titles listed in the computer. Macy enters 292 new titles. To find the total number of CDs listed now, which operation would you use?

   (A) addition

   (B) subtraction

   (C) multiplication

   (D) division

2. This map shows Janelle's yard. She came in through the gate and walked three yards in one direction, then turned and went two yards in a different direction. She ended up closest to the steps. In which direction can you predict that she traveled?

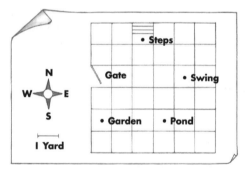

   (F) east and north

   (G) south and east

   (H) west and south

   (J) north and west

3. Kat, Eddy, Carter, and Meena stand in line. Meena and Kat stand next to each other. Meena is behind Carter. Eddy is not first. There is one person in between Meena and Eddy. In which order are the friends standing in line?

   (A) Eddy, Carter, Meena, Kat

   (B) Carter, Meena, Kat, Eddy

   (C) Carter, Eddy, Meena, Kat

   (D) Kat, Eddy, Carter, Meena

4. There are 120 sheets of construction paper in a package. Ms. Claus's class uses 16 one week, 42 the next week, and 30 the following week. How many pieces are left?

   (F) 18

   (G) 30

   (H) 42

   (J) 32

5. Emma made a rectangular painting that measures 12 inches on one side and 16 inches on another. Emma wants to frame it for her mom. What will the perimeter of the frame need to be?

   (A) 32 inches

   (B) 56 inches

   (C) 24 inches

   (D) 192 inches

Name _____ Date _____

Solving Word Problems

Directions: Read and work each problem. Find the correct answer. Fill in the circle.

1. There were 485 balloons decorating the gymnasium for a party. There were 97 students at the party. Each student brought home an equal number of balloons after the party. What operation would you use to find out how many balloons each student brought home?

   Ⓐ addition

   Ⓑ subtraction

   Ⓒ multiplication

   Ⓓ division

2. How many balloons did each student in question 1 bring home?

   Ⓕ 3 balloons

   Ⓖ 4 balloons

   Ⓗ 5 balloons

   Ⓙ 6 balloons

3. A plane has 124 passengers, 3 pilots, and 9 flight attendants. What is the total number of people on the plane?

   Ⓐ 136 people

   Ⓑ 135 people

   Ⓒ 133 people

   Ⓓ 112 people

4. A babysitter works for 4 hours and earns $20. Which number sentence shows how to find the amount of money the babysitter earns in one hour?

   Ⓕ $4 \times \$20 = \square$

   Ⓖ $\$5 + \square = \$20$

   Ⓗ $\$20 \div 4 = \square$

   Ⓙ $4 \div \square = \$20$

5. CJ wants to buy 3 bottles of juice at the grocery store. Each bottle costs $0.95. How much will 3 bottles of juice cost?

   Ⓐ $3.00

   Ⓑ $2.85

   Ⓒ $2.75

   Ⓓ $2.50

6. Desiree measured a piece of fabric that was 1 foot, 10 inches long. How many inches total was it?

   Ⓕ 12 inches

   Ⓖ 20 inches

   Ⓗ 24 inches

   Ⓙ 22 inches

Name _____ Date _____

Solving Word Problems

Directions: Read and work each problem. Find the correct answer. Fill in the circle.

1. Mrs. Hobbs is planting her vegetable garden. She has 48 plants. She plans to put 8 plants in each row. Which number sentence could you use to find out how many rows she will have?

   Ⓐ $48 \times \square = 8$

   Ⓑ $8 \times 48 = \square$

   Ⓒ $\square + 8 = 48$

   Ⓓ $48 \div 8 = \square$

2. Erin is riding her bike across the state to raise money for an animal shelter. She has ridden 139 miles so far. If you want to know how much farther she has to ride, what piece of information do you need to know?

   Ⓕ how fast she rides

   Ⓖ how many miles she rides per day

   Ⓗ the total length of the trip

   Ⓙ how many miles she rides per week

3. In the picture below, 1 fish stands for 10 fish. How many fish does this picture stand for?

   Ⓐ 8

   Ⓑ 80

   Ⓒ 10

   Ⓓ 60

4. Antoine measured a board that was 4 inches long. Three boards laid end to end would measure _____ long.

   Ⓕ 1 foot

   Ⓖ 2 feet

   Ⓗ 10 inches

   Ⓙ 16 inches

5. Nick has been mowing lawns and saving his money. During the summer, he earned $35 a week for 9 weeks. Which number sentence shows how to find how much money he earned?

   Ⓐ $\$35 \div 9 = \square$

   Ⓑ $\$35 \times 9 = \square$

   Ⓒ $9 \times \square = \$35$

   Ⓓ $\$35 - \square = 9$

Name _____ Date _____

Solving Word Problems

Directions: Read and work each problem. Find the correct answer. Fill in the circle.

1. **Trey weighs 68 pounds. Bella weighs 5 pounds more than Trey and 2 pounds less than James. How much does James weigh?**

   Ⓐ 67 pounds

   Ⓑ 72 pounds

   Ⓒ 75 pounds

   Ⓓ 73 pounds

2. **Mr. Campbell has a booth at the farmers' market. He has 32 baskets and wants to put 9 peaches in each basket. Which number sentence shows how to find how many peaches he has altogether?**

   Ⓕ □ ÷ 9 = 32

   Ⓖ 32 × 9 = □

   Ⓗ 32 + 9 = □

   Ⓙ 9 × □ = 32

Directions: Use the information in the box to answer the questions that follow.

☀ **Summer Sale!** ☀

All Swimsuits	$14.99
Beach Towels	$8.99
Flip-Flops	$2.99
Goggles	$2.50
Sunscreen	$3.50

4. **Eduardo bought a new swimsuit. He paid for it with a $20 bill. How much change did he receive?**

   Ⓕ $4.99

   Ⓖ $5.01

   Ⓗ $2.01

   Ⓙ $5.99

3. **How much would a swimsuit, a pair of flip-flops, and some sunscreen cost?**

   Ⓐ $21.48

   Ⓑ $17.98

   Ⓒ $20.48

   Ⓓ $22.98

5. **Mrs. Fishburn bought a beach towel for each of her three daughters. Which number sentence shows how to find her total cost?**

   Ⓐ $8.99 + 3 = □

   Ⓑ $8.99 + $8.99 = □

   Ⓒ $8.99 ÷ 3 = □

   Ⓓ $8.99 × 3 = □

Organizing and Displaying Data

Directions: Read and work each problem. Find the correct answer. Fill in the circle.

Tia was helping out in her dad's shoe store. She thinks that the store sells more of some sizes than others. Answer the questions below about how Tia can find out if this is true.

1. **What could Tia do to find out what size shoes are sold each day?**

   Ⓐ Ask everyone in the store what size shoe they wear.

   Ⓑ Count all the shoe boxes at the end of every day.

   Ⓒ Find the average number of customers in the store each day.

   Ⓓ Make a tally of the size of each pair of shoes as they are sold.

2. **This is Tia's tally for the first day. What can Tia find out from this tally?**

Tally for 1st Day	
Size	**Tally**
5	//
6	////
7	///
8	///
9	/

   Ⓕ the color of the shoes sold

   Ⓖ how many pairs of shoes each customer bought

   Ⓗ the size of each pair of shoes sold

   Ⓙ how many boxes of shoes the store owns

3. **These are Tia's tallies for the second and third days. Fill in the table to show the total number of shoes sold in each size for all three days. The first day's tallies are in question 2.**

Tally for 2nd Day	
Size	**Tally**
5	/
6	////
7	//
8	/
9	

Tally for 3rd Day	
Size	**Tally**
5	//
6	ЖЖ
7	///
8	//
9	/

Shoe Size	Total Pairs Sold
5	
6	
7	
8	
9	

Name _____ Date _____

Organizing and Displaying Data

Directions: Read and work each problem. Find the correct answer. Fill in the circle.

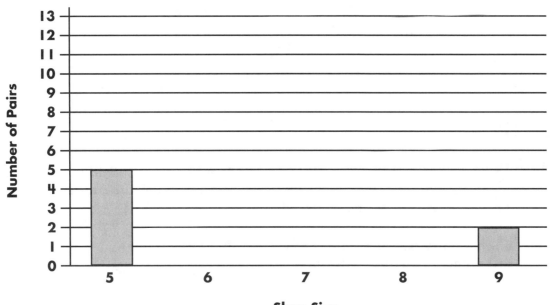

Shoe Size

4. **Add the bars missing from the graph to show the number of shoes sold in each size.**

5. **What does Tia know from all of the information she has gathered?**

   (A) More size 5 shoes were sold.

   (B) More size 6 shoes were sold.

   (C) More size 7 shoes were sold.

   (D) More size 8 shoes were sold.

6. **Look at the table you completed in question 3. Arrange the numbers for the total pairs sold in order from least to greatest. What is the median for the total pairs of shoes that were sold?**

   (F) 5

   (G) 6

   (H) 8

   (J) 12

7. **What can Tia predict now?**

   (A) The black shoes are the most popular.

   (B) More customers wear size 6 than other sizes.

   (C) More customers wear size 9 than other sizes.

   (D) None of these

   The median is the number in the middle when a group of numbers is arranged in order from least to greatest.

Ready to Test • Third Grade

Organizing and Displaying Data

Directions: Study the graph. Use the information to answer the questions that follow.

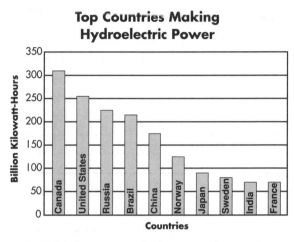

Top Countries Making Hydroelectric Power

1. **Which country below produces the least amount of hydroelectricity?**

   Ⓐ Brazil

   Ⓑ China

   Ⓒ India

   Ⓓ Canada

2. **Which country produces more hydroelectricity than Brazil but less than the U.S.?**

   Ⓕ Russia

   Ⓖ China

   Ⓗ Canada

   Ⓙ Brazil

3. **Which country below produces the most hydroelectricity?**

   Ⓐ India

   Ⓑ France

   Ⓒ Canada

   Ⓓ Russia

4. **About how much hydroelectricity does Norway produce?**

   Ⓕ 100 billion kilowatt-hours

   Ⓖ 125 billion kilowatt-hours

   Ⓗ 150 billion kilowatt-hours

   Ⓙ 200 billion kilowatt-hours

5. **In which class would a graph like this most likely be used?**

   Ⓐ geography

   Ⓑ music

   Ⓒ English

   Ⓓ gym

6. **Which statement is not true?**

   Ⓕ Brazil produces less than 200 billion kilowatt-hours.

   Ⓖ Russia produces about 225 billion kilowatt-hours.

   Ⓗ Canada produces more than 300 billion kilowatt-hours.

   Ⓙ India produces about 75 billion kilowatt-hours.

Organizing and Displaying Data

Directions: Frost Elementary sold fruit baskets to help raise money for a new gym. Study the graph of the students' sales. Use the information to answer the questions that follow.

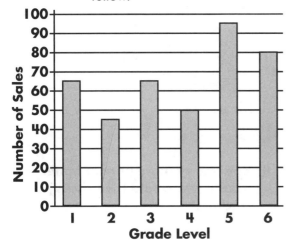

1. What does this graph show?

Ⓐ the amount of money each grade level raised

Ⓑ the number of students in each grade level

Ⓒ the number of fruit baskets sold by grade level

Ⓓ the number of students who sold fruit baskets

2. How many fruit baskets did the fourth grade sell?

Ⓕ 45 baskets

Ⓖ 50 baskets

Ⓗ 55 baskets

Ⓙ 65 baskets

3. Which two grade levels sold the same number of baskets?

Ⓐ first and third

Ⓑ third and fourth

Ⓒ first and second

Ⓓ second and fourth

4. How many combined baskets did the fourth, fifth, and sixth grades sell?

Ⓕ 200 baskets

Ⓖ 225 baskets

Ⓗ 250 baskets

Ⓙ 275 baskets

5. Which grade level sold the fewest fruit baskets?

Ⓐ Grade 1

Ⓑ Grade 2

Ⓒ Grade 3

Ⓓ Grade 4

6. Which number sentence shows how to find how many more baskets the sixth grade sold than the third grade?

Ⓕ $80 - 65 = \square$

Ⓖ $80 - \square = 65$

Ⓗ $80 + 65 = \square$

Ⓙ $80 \div \square = 65$

Organizing and Displaying Data

Directions: The table below shows the number of treats that were sold last weekend at Buster's Dog Bakery. Use the table to answer the questions that follow.

Dog Treat	Number of Items Sold
peanut butter biscuits	🦴🦴🦴🦴🦴🦴🦴🦴🦴
tuna treats	🦴🦴🦴🦴🦴
cheesy crackers	🦴🦴🦴🦴🦴🦴
beefy bites	🦴🦴🦴🦴
fresh-breath cookies	🦴🦴
meatloaf nuggets	🦴🦴🦴🦴

Key

each 🦴 = 5 items

1. **The bakery sold equal amounts of which two types of treats?**

   (A) beefy bites and fresh-breath cookies

   (B) tuna treats and cheesy crackers

   (C) beefy bites and meatloaf nuggets

   (D) meatloaf nuggets and
       fresh-breath cookies

2. **How many tuna treats and cheesy crackers did they sell altogether?**

   (F) 14

   (G) 70

   (H) 30

   (J) 40

3. **The bakery sold fewer _____ than any other type of treat.**

   (A) peanut butter biscuits

   (B) beefy bites

   (C) tuna treats

   (D) fresh-breath cookies

4. **How many more peanut butter biscuits were sold than cheesy crackers?**

   (F) 15

   (G) 9

   (H) 3

   (J) 11

5. **Which list below shows the number of treats sold from least to greatest?**

   (A) peanut butter biscuits, cheesy crackers, tuna treats, beefy bites, meatloaf nuggets, fresh-breath cookies

   (B) fresh-breath cookies, meatloaf nuggets, beefy bites, tuna treats, cheesy crackers, peanut butter biscuits

   (C) tuna treats, peanut butter biscuits, meatloaf nuggets, cheesy crackers, beefy bites, fresh-breath cookies

   (D) fresh-breath cookies, meatloaf nuggets, beefy bites, cheesy crackers, tuna treats, peanut butter biscuits

Organizing and Displaying Data

Directions: The third-grade students at Zinser Elementary were asked to do reports on one of the following birds: hummingbird, hawk, owl, blue jay, or California condor. Use the pie graph below to answer questions 1–3.

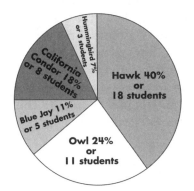

1. Which of the following lists the birds from least to most favorite?

Ⓐ hawk, owl, California condor, blue jay, hummingbird

Ⓑ blue jay, hummingbird, California condor, owl, hawk

Ⓒ California condor, hawk, owl, blue jay, hummingbird

Ⓓ hummingbird, blue jay, California condor, owl, hawk

2. Which two kinds of birds combined got more than 50 percent of the vote?

Ⓕ hawk and owl

Ⓖ hummingbird and California condor

Ⓗ hummingbird and blue jay

Ⓙ hawk and hummingbird

3. What percent of the vote do the hummingbird, California condor, and blue jay make up together?

Ⓐ 40%

Ⓑ 25%

Ⓒ 30%

Ⓓ 36%

4. Sarah just read that her town has the highest population in the county. Based on the chart below, in which town does Sarah live?

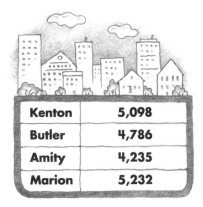

Kenton	5,098
Butler	4,786
Amity	4,235
Marion	5,232

Ⓕ Kenton

Ⓖ Butler

Ⓗ Amity

Ⓙ Marion

5. Based on the chart in question 5, which town has the lowest population?

Ⓐ Kenton

Ⓑ Butler

Ⓒ Amity

Ⓓ Marion

MATH
230

Sample Test 11: Applications

Directions: Read and work each problem. Find the correct answer. Fill in the circle.

1. Which combination of coins makes $0.40?

- (A) 1 nickel, 1 dime, 1 half-dollar
- (B) 2 dimes, 1 nickel, 5 pennies
- (C) 3 dimes, 1 nickel, 1 penny
- (D) 1 nickel, 1 dime, 1 quarter

2. How many bicycles and cars would you need to have a total of 26 wheels?

- (F) 6 cars and 1 bicycle
- (G) 5 cars and 2 bicycles
- (H) 4 cars and 3 bicycles
- (J) 2 cars and 7 bicycles

3. Preston is 9 centimeters shorter than Stewart. If Stewart is 122 centimeters tall, Preston is

- (A) 112 centimeters tall.
- (B) 111 centimeters tall.
- (C) 113 centimeters tall.
- (D) 103 centimeters tall.

4. Which of these numbers would round to 300?

- (F) 226
- (G) 249
- (H) 252
- (J) 239

5. Cody played in 3 basketball games. In the first game, he scored 17 points. In the second game, he scored 22 points. In the third game, he scored twice as many points as in his first game. His points for the third game totaled

- (A) 34.
- (B) 36.
- (C) 44.
- (D) 42.

6. On Saturday, Hiro took 12 pictures. On Sunday, he took 24 pictures. If it costs $0.20 per print, how much will it be for Hiro to have prints made of all his pictures?

- (F) $2.40
- (G) $4.80
- (H) $7.20
- (J) $6.80

Preview the test before you begin. That way, you'll know how to budget your time. You'll also know what to expect!

GO

Sample Test 11: Applications

Directions: Read and work each problem. Find the correct answer. Fill in the circle.

Use the prices in the box below to answer questions 7–10.

Family Tent $90.00
Two Person Tent .... _____
Sleeping Bags $16.00
Cooking Stove $25.00
Cooking Sets $23.00
  (dishes, pots)
Cutlery $15.00

7. How much would a family tent and 4 sleeping bags cost?

- (A) $154.00
- (B) $152.00
- (C) $90.00
- (D) $64.00

8. The two-person tent costs $\frac{1}{3}$ the price of the family tent. It costs

- (F) $20.00
- (G) $30.00
- (H) $60.00
- (J) $70.00

9. Which is the cheapest to buy?

- (A) 1 family tent and 2 sleeping bags
- (B) 2 two-person tents and 2 sleeping bags
- (C) 4 sleeping bags and 1 cooking stove
- (D) 1 family tent and 1 cooking stove

10. If you bought 1 cooking stove, 1 cooking set, and 1 set of cutlery, you would pay

- (F) $60.00.
- (G) $62.00.
- (H) $63.00.
- (J) $59.00.

11. A waiter put 9 napkins on each table. There were 9 tables total. The waiter used

- (A) 72 napkins.
- (B) 81 napkins.
- (C) 96 napkins.
- (D) 99 napkins.

12. There are 167 students in Nita's grade at school. Seventy-one of the students are girls. How many are boys?

- (F) 90
- (G) 98
- (H) 96
- (J) 106

MATH
232

Sample Test 11: Applications

Directions: Read and work each problem. Find the correct answer. Fill in the circle.

13. One letter is randomly chosen from the word *remembered*. What are the chances the letter will be an *e*?

(A) 4 out of 4

(B) 4 out of 10

(C) 2 out of 10

(D) 1 out of 10

14. A number cube is rolled. What is the probability of rolling a 5 or a 6?

(F) 1 out of 6

(G) 2 out of 6

(H) 5 out of 6

(J) 6 out of 6

15. Jin flipped a coin 3 times. Each time he flipped it, what were the chances of the coin coming up heads?

(A) 0

(B) 1 out of 1

(C) 1 out of 2

(D) 2 out of 2

16. Alexi received a bunch of balloons for her birthday. There were 4 pink balloons, 3 green balloons, 3 white balloons, and 2 yellow balloons. If Alexi randomly pulls one string, what are the chances she'll pull out a green balloon?

(F) 4 out of 12

(G) 3 out of 3

(H) 3 out of 6

(J) 3 out of 12

17. What color balloon is Alexi least likely to pull out?

(A) pink

(B) yellow

(C) white

(D) green

18. What two colors of balloons is Alexi equally likely to choose?

(F) pink and green

(G) pink and white

(H) green and white

(J) white and yellow

GO

Sample Test 11: Applications

Directions: Use the tally chart to answer the questions that follow.

Favorite Hobbies	
bike riding	Жℋ //
reading	Жℋ ///
sports	Жℋ Жℋ /
arts/crafts	Жℋ /
animals	Жℋ
music	///

19. From how many students was the data collected?

(A) 30

(B) 38

(C) 42

(D) 40

20. Which number sentence shows how to find the answer to question 19?

(F) 7 + 8 + 11 + 6 + 5 = ☐

(G) 7 × 8 × 11 × 6 × 5 × 3 = ☐

(H) 7 + 8 + 11 + 6 + 5 + 3 = ☐

(J) 7 − 8 − 11 − 6 − 5 − 3 = ☐

21. How many more students chose sports than music?

(A) 11

(B) 8

(C) 3

(D) 7

22. Which list shows the hobbies in order from least to most popular?

(F) music, animals, arts/crafts, bike riding, reading, sports

(G) sports, reading, bike riding, arts/crafts, animals, music

(H) music, animals, arts/crafts, sports, reading, bike riding

(J) bike riding, reading, sports, arts/crafts, animals, music

23. Five more students chose music as their favorite hobby. What should the tally marks for music look like now?

(A) Жℋ

(B) ///

(C) Жℋ ///

(D) Жℋ ////

24. How many more students chose reading than arts/crafts?

(F) 2

(G) 3

(H) 5

(J) 1

STOP

Name _____ Date _____

Practice Test 3: Math
Part 1: Concepts

Directions: Read and work each problem. Find the correct answer. Fill in the circle.

1. You are number 11 in a line of 30 people. How many people are ahead of you?

- (A) 19
- (B) 11
- (C) 10
- (D) 20

2. What is another name for 4 hundreds, 2 tens, and 8 ones?

- (F) 284
- (G) 482
- (H) 428
- (J) 824

3. Which number is less than 807?

- (A) 806
- (B) 808
- (C) 809
- (D) 810

4. How many tens are in 1,525?

- (F) 5
- (G) 6
- (H) 2
- (J) 1

5. What number is represented by the chart?

Hundreds	Tens	Ones
I I I I I	I I I	I I I I I I I

- (A) 737
- (B) 573
- (C) 436
- (D) 537

6. Look at the number pattern in the box. Find the number that is missing.

| 11 | 22 | ____ | 44 | 55 |

- (F) 33
- (G) 23
- (H) 66
- (J) 42

7. Which number is more than 432?

- (A) 442
- (B) 423
- (C) 342
- (D) 234

8. How many ones are in 7,819?

- (F) 8
- (G) 9
- (H) 7
- (J) 1

GO ▶

Practice Test 3: Math
Part 1: Concepts

Directions: Read and work each problem. Find the correct answer. Fill in the circle.

9. The pattern is apple, pear, banana, orange. Which is the missing piece of fruit in the third row?

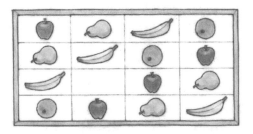

Ⓐ orange

Ⓑ pear

Ⓒ banana

Ⓓ apple

10. Round 6,679 to the nearest thousand.

Ⓕ 6,000

Ⓖ 6,700

Ⓗ 7,000

Ⓙ 7,600

11. From the figures below, you know that

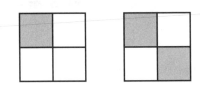

Ⓐ $\frac{1}{4}$ is greater than $\frac{4}{8}$.

Ⓑ $\frac{4}{8}$ is greater than $\frac{4}{8}$.

Ⓒ $\frac{4}{8}$ is greater than $\frac{4}{8}$.

Ⓓ $\frac{4}{8}$ is greater than $\frac{4}{8}$.

12. Count by tens. Which number comes after 40 and before 60?

Ⓕ 50

Ⓖ 80

Ⓗ 100

Ⓙ 60

13. Which of these fractions is the largest?

Ⓐ $\frac{4}{5}$

Ⓑ $\frac{1}{2}$

Ⓒ $\frac{3}{4}$

Ⓓ $\frac{2}{5}$

14. Which number is an even number and can be divided evenly by 9?

Ⓕ 24

Ⓖ 36

Ⓗ 81

Ⓙ 40

15. Which group of numbers has four even numbers?

Ⓐ 9, 12, 15, 17, 21, 26, 33

Ⓑ 7, 10, 12, 13, 18, 22, 37

Ⓒ 2, 5, 8, 14, 19, 25, 31, 41

Ⓓ 16, 27, 28, 29, 30, 35, 39

16. 27 + □ = 30
    10 − □ = 7
    Which number completes both number sentences above?

Ⓕ 3

Ⓖ 4

Ⓗ 5

Ⓙ 7

Practice Test 3: Math
Part 1: Concepts

Directions: Read and work each problem. Find the correct answer. Fill in the circle.

17. Which number sentence shows the total number of beans?

- Ⓐ 18 + 2
- Ⓑ 30 ÷ 2
- Ⓒ 10 − 2
- Ⓓ 3 × 4

18. 71 − ☐ = 51
19 + ☐ = 39
Which number completes both number sentences above?

- Ⓕ 23
- Ⓖ 20
- Ⓗ 32
- Ⓙ 30

19. Which of these is closest in value to 9,000?

- Ⓐ 8,972
- Ⓑ 8,991
- Ⓒ 8,003
- Ⓓ 8,011

20. Which of these is 622 rounded to the nearest hundred?

- Ⓕ 600
- Ⓖ 620
- Ⓗ 700
- Ⓙ 720

21. Round these numbers to the nearest hundred: 514, 559, 460, 421, 487, 551. How many of them will be 500?

- Ⓐ 3
- Ⓑ 4
- Ⓒ 5
- Ⓓ 6

22. $\frac{2}{3} = \frac{\Box}{6}$
What does the ☐ equal?

- Ⓕ 2
- Ⓖ 5
- Ⓗ 4
- Ⓙ 6

23. Which of these is closest in value to 200?

- Ⓐ 189
- Ⓑ 198
- Ⓒ 209
- Ⓓ 290

GO ▶

Name _____   Date _____

Practice Test 3: Math
Part 1: Concepts

Directions: Read and work each problem. Find the correct answer. Fill in the circle.

24. How can you write 3,776 in expanded notation?

(F) 3,000 + 700 + 70 + 6

(G) 3,000 + 700 + 76

(H) 3 + 7 + 7 + 6

(J) 3,000 + 776

25. What is another name for 5 hundreds, 0 tens, and 6 ones?

(A) 5,006

(B) 506

(C) 560

(D) 605

26. What is another way to write 6,425?

(F) 6 hundreds, 4 tens, and 25 ones

(G) 6 thousands, 4 hundreds, and 5 ones

(H) 6 thousands, 4 hundreds, 2 tens, and 5 ones

(J) 5 thousands, 2 hundreds, 4 tens, and 6 ones

27. How many hundreds are in 4,217?

(A) 7

(B) 1

(C) 2

(D) 4

Directions: Look for a pattern in the IN and OUT numbers in each table. Decide which function you need to use to get from each IN number to the OUT number below it. Fill in the table. Then, write the rule for getting from the IN number to the OUT number.

28.

IN	6	18	22	50	64	_____	90
OUT	3	9	11	_____	32	44	_____

Rule: _____

29.

IN	7	12	65	29	43	18	_____
OUT	4	9	_____	26	_____	15	53

Rule: _____

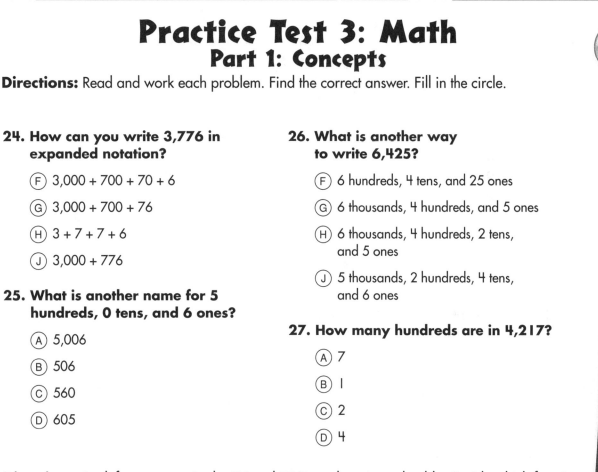

GO

Practice Test 3: Math

Ready to Test • Third Grade

Practice Test 3: Math
Part 1: Concepts

Directions: Read and work each problem. Find the correct answer. Fill in the circle.

30. What number makes this number sentence true?

$\square \div 6 = 8$

(F) 36

(G) 64

(H) 48

(J) 52

31. What number makes this number sentence true?

$\square + 5 = 18$

(A) 13

(B) 15

(C) 12

(D) 16

32. What number makes this number sentence true?

$\square \times 11 = 44$

(F) 11

(G) 4

(H) 14

(J) 41

Directions: Choose the equation that best describes the text.

33. Mr. and Mrs. Jackson run a pet-sitting business. They have 19 pets to take care of today. They have visited 8 pets so far. How many pets do they still need to care for?

(A) $19 - 8 = \square$

(B) $19 \div 8 = \square$

(C) $19 \times \square = 8$

(D) $19 + \square = 8$

34. A helium balloon costs $1.59. How much do 12 balloons cost?

(F) $\$1.59 \times 12 = \square$

(G) $\$1.59 \div 12 = \square$

(H) $\$1.59 + 12 = \square$

(J) $\$1.59 \times \square = 12$

35. Kerry has 128 stickers in her sticker collection. She wants to give the stickers to her 8 cousins. How many stickers will each cousin get?

(A) $128 \times \square = 8$

(B) $8 + \square = 128$

(C) $128 \div 8 = \square$

(D) $128 + 8 = \square$

STOP

Practice Test 3: Math
Part 2: Computation

Directions: Mark the space for the correct answer to each problem. Choose "None of these" if the correct answer is not given.

1. 321
   - 75

   (A) 246

   (B) 396

   (C) 386

   (D) None of these

2. $\frac{4}{7} - \frac{3}{7} =$

   (F) $\frac{2}{7}$

   (G) $\frac{3}{7}$

   (H) $\frac{1}{7}$

   (J) None of these

3. $\frac{7}{10} - \frac{3}{10} =$

   (A) $\frac{5}{10}$

   (B) $\frac{4}{10}$

   (C) $\frac{3}{10}$

   (D) None of these

4. 25 + 25 + 6 =

   (F) 51

   (G) 56

   (H) 61

   (J) None of these

5. 3,000
   +1,350

   (A) 1,650

   (B) 4,350

   (C) 4,400

   (D) None of these

6. 2.99
   +1.15

   (F) 4.16

   (G) 4.14

   (H) 4.15

   (J) None of these

7. 622
   +222

   (A) 844

   (B) 400

   (C) 422

   (D) None of these

8. 15 – 9 =

   (F) 5

   (G) 6

   (H) 7

   (J) None of these

9. 35 + 21 + 9 =

   (A) 55

   (B) 60

   (C) 65

   (D) None of these

10. $7.19 – $2.20 =

   (F) $9.39

   (G) $9.99

   (H) $5.99

   (J) None of these

GO

Practice Test 3: Math
Part 2: Computation

Directions: Mark the space for the correct answer to each problem. Choose "None of these" if the correct answer is not given.

11.   551
     + 17
   (A) 568
   (B) 578
   (C) 534
   (D) None of these

12.   5,670
     + 128
   (F) 5,799
   (G) 5,797
   (H) 5,796
   (J) None of these

13. $\frac{4}{5} - \frac{1}{5} =$
   (A) $\frac{3}{10}$
   (B) $\frac{3}{5}$
   (C) $\frac{1}{5}$
   (D) None of these

14. $5\overline{)200}$
   (F) 50
   (G) 40
   (H) 30
   (J) None of these

15.   4,009
     −   35
   (A) 3,994
   (B) 4,044
   (C) 3,974
   (D) None of these

16.   0.98
     − 0.29
   (F) 1.27
   (G) 0.79
   (H) 0.69
   (J) None of these

17.   77
     × 6
   (A) 472
   (B) 460
   (C) 464
   (D) None of these

18. $6\overline{)62}$
   (F) 10 R1
   (G) 10
   (H) 10 R2
   (J) None of these

19. $1\frac{3}{4} - \frac{1}{4} =$
   (A) $1\frac{2}{4}$
   (B) $1\frac{3}{4}$
   (C) $1\frac{5}{4}$
   (D) None of these

20. $4.25 − $1.15 =$
   (F) $4.40
   (G) $5.40
   (H) $3.10
   (J) None of these

GO ▶

Practice Test 3: Math
Part 2: Computation

Directions: Mark the space for the correct answer to each problem. Choose "None of these" if the correct answer is not given.

21. $48 \div 6 = \square$
   $6 \times \square = 48$

   (A) 6

   (B) 8

   (C) 12

   (D) None of these

22. $140 \div 10 = \square$
   $10 \times \square = 140$

   (F) 8

   (G) 10

   (H) 14

   (J) None of these

23. $9 \times \square = 72$
   $72 \div 9 = \square$

   (A) 7

   (B) 9

   (C) 24

   (D) None of these

24. $9 \times \square = 45$
   $45 \div \square = 9$

   (F) 5

   (G) 7

   (H) 9

   (J) None of these

25. Suppose you want to estimate how to find 62 + 29 to the nearest ten. Which of these number sentences would you use?

   (A) 60 + 20

   (B) 60 + 30

   (C) 70 + 30

   (D) None of these

26. Reiko loves to draw. He made 13 drawings in July, 26 in August, and 18 in September. Which of these estimates is closest to the total number of drawings Reiko did?

   (F) 50

   (G) 60

   (H) 70

   (J) None of these

27. Which of these is the best way to estimate the answer to this problem?
   $82 \div 18 = \square$

   (A) $80 \div 20$

   (B) $90 \div 20$

   (C) $80 \div 10$

   (D) None of these

28. Use estimation to find which of these number sentences is closest to 60.

   (F) 67 − 19

   (G) $362 \div 54$

   (H) 38 + 16

   (J) 64 − 24

STOP

Practice Test 3: Math
Part 3: Geometry, Measurement, and Applications

Directions: Read and work each problem. Find the correct answer. Fill in the circle.

1. Tania had a rectangle made out of paper. She drew a line down the middle of the rectangle, and then she drew a diagonal line through the rectangle. She then had four shapes. What is one shape she made?

   (A) square

   (B) circle

   (C) triangle

   (D) oval

2. $\frac{2}{3}$ ☐ $\frac{3}{2}$

   Choose the correct symbol to go in the box.

   (F) <

   (G) >

   (H) =

   (J) Not enough information

3. Which of these is symmetrical?

   (A) **U**

   (B) **L**

   (C) **K**

   (D) **Q**

Use the graph to answer questions 4 and 5.

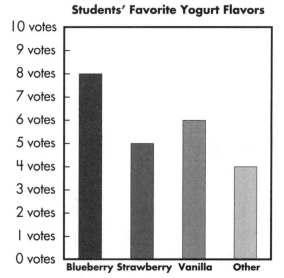

Students' Favorite Yogurt Flavors

4. How many students named vanilla as their favorite?

   (F) 2

   (G) 6

   (H) 8

   (J) Not enough information

5. How many more students voted for blueberry yogurt than for strawberry?

   (A) 3

   (B) 8

   (C) 13

   (D) Not enough information

GO

Practice Test 3: Math
Part 3: Geometry, Measurement, and Applications

Directions: Read and work each problem. Find the correct answer. Fill in the circle.

6. Look at the clock. How long will it take the minute hand to reach the 6?

- Ⓕ 3 minutes
- Ⓖ 5 minutes
- Ⓗ 12 minutes
- Ⓙ 15 minutes

7. What unit of weight would be best to weigh a young child?

- Ⓐ ounces
- Ⓑ pints
- Ⓒ pounds
- Ⓓ tons

Use the calendar to answer questions 8–10.

April

Sunday	Monday	Tuesday	Wednesday	Thursday	Friday	Saturday
				1	2	3
4	5	6	7	8	9	10
11	12	13	14	15	16	17
18	19	20	21	22	23	24
25	26	27	28	29	30	

8. Mr. and Mrs. Akers are going to build a deck. It will take two weeks to finish. They plan to start on April 7. What date will they finish?

- Ⓕ April 24
- Ⓖ April 21
- Ⓗ April 14
- Ⓙ April 23

9. Mrs. Akers is going to plant flowers around the new deck. She plans to buy the flowers on April 24 and be done in 2 days. What are the days of the week on which she will be planting flowers?

- Ⓐ Friday and Saturday
- Ⓑ Saturday and Sunday
- Ⓒ Sunday and Monday
- Ⓓ Not enough information

10. Mr. and Mrs. Gupta are leaving on a trip on Monday, April 26. If they are returning the following Saturday, on which date will they return?

- Ⓕ April 30
- Ⓖ April 27
- Ⓗ May 1
- Ⓙ May 2

11. Mr. Simms has 4 boxes. There are 16 candles in each box. Mr. Simms wants to use all of the candles and put an equal number on each of 8 tables. How many candles will be on each table?

- Ⓐ 64 candles
- Ⓑ 8 candles
- Ⓒ 32 candles
- Ⓓ 56 candles

Practice Test 3: Math
Part 3: Geometry, Measurement, and Applications

Directions: Read and work each problem. Find the correct answer. Fill in the circle.

12. Which word describes how the figure below was moved?

G Ɔ

- (F) rotation
- (G) reflection
- (H) symmetry
- (J) None of these

13. Which of these objects is a cone?

(A)

(B)

(C)

(D)

Directions: The points **M**, **N**, and **O** represent the houses of three friends—Matt, Nate, and Onan. Each square in the grid represents a square mile. The heavy black lines represent roads. Use the following grid to answer questions 14–16.

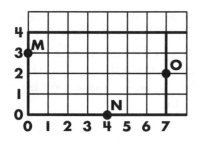

15. What is the location of Nate's house?

- (A) (1, 1)
- (B) (0, 3)
- (C) (4, 0)
- (D) (7, 2)

14. What is the location of Matt's house?

- (F) (1, 1)
- (G) (0, 3)
- (H) (4, 0)
- (J) (7, 2)

16. What is the location of Onan's house?

- (F) (1, 1)
- (G) (0, 3)
- (H) (4, 0)
- (J) (7, 2)

GO

Practice Test 3: Math
Part 3: Geometry, Measurement, and Applications

Directions: Fill in the blanks with the equivalent measurement. Use the chart below to help you.

> ## 1 foot = 12 inches
> ## 1 yard = 3 feet
> ## 1 mile = 5,280 feet

17. 1 yard 12 inches = _____ feet

- (A) 3
- (B) 4
- (C) 5
- (D) 6

18. 14 feet = _____ inches

- (F) 124
- (G) 140
- (H) 148
- (J) 168

19. 4 miles = _____ feet

- (A) 1,320
- (B) 15,840
- (C) 21,120
- (D) 22,200

Directions: Use the following information to answer questions 20–22. Fill in the circle.

There are 8 gold paperclips, 7 silver paperclips, and 3 white paperclips in a basket.

20. What color clip is Louisa least likely to pull out of the basket?

- (F) gold
- (G) silver
- (H) white
- (J) Not enough information

21. What are the chances that Louisa will pull a silver clip out of the basket?

- (A) $\frac{7}{8}$
- (B) $\frac{7}{7}$
- (C) $\frac{7}{18}$
- (D) $\frac{10}{22}$

22. What are the chances that Louisa will pull a gold clip out of the basket?

- (F) $\frac{8}{18}$
- (G) $\frac{8}{15}$
- (H) $\frac{7}{18}$
- (J) $\frac{3}{7}$

GO

Practice Test 3: Math
Part 3: Geometry, Measurement, and Applications

Directions: Read and work each problem. Find the correct answer. Fill in the circle.

23. One letter is randomly chosen from the word *appearance*. Which letter has a 3 out of 10 chance of being chosen?

(A) e

(B) a

(C) p

(D) c

24. One letter is randomly chosen from the word *attraction*. Which letter is more likely to be chosen than *n* but less likely to be chosen than *t*?

(F) o

(G) i

(H) r

(J) a

Directions: Use the pie graph below to answer the questions that follow. Fill in the circle.

Dog Breeds at the Happy Hounds Dog Rescue

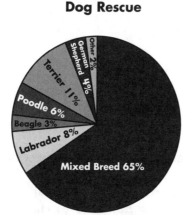

Other 2%
German Shepherd 4%
Terrier 11%
Poodle 6%
Beagle 3%
Labrador 8%
Mixed Breed 65%

25. What percentage of the dogs are either beagle, poodle, or terrier?

(A) 26%

(B) 22%

(C) 20%

(D) 18%

26. What percentage of the dogs are German shepherds?

(F) 6%

(G) 2%

(H) 3%

(J) 4%

27. Which statement is not true?

(A) There are 3 times as many Labradors as German shepherds.

(B) There are fewer beagles than Labradors.

(C) There are more terriers than poodles at the rescue.

(D) Most of the dogs at the rescue are mixed breed.

28. If there were 100 dogs at the rescue, how many would be poodles?

(F) 6 out of 100

(G) 16 out of 100

(H) 6 out of 10

(J) 60 out of 100

page 9
1. B
2. F
3. D
4. G
5. C
6. G

page 10
1. A
2. J
3. C
4. J
5. B
6. F

page 11
1. D
2. H
3. B
4. G
5. D
6. J

page 12
1. A
2. H
3. B
4. G
5. B
6. F
7. D
8. G
9. A
10. G

page 13
1. C
2. J
3. C
4. G
5. D
6. F

page 14
1. A
2. J
3. B
4. G
5. C

page 15
1. D
2. G
3. C
4. H
5. A
6. J

page 16
1. C
2. J
3. B
4. G
5. A
6. H

page 17
1. C
2. J
3. A
4. F

page 18
1. A
2. G
3. B
4. F

page 19
1. D
2. H
3. A
4. G
5. D
6. G
7. A
8. H

page 20
9. A
10. J
11. B
12. J
13. B
14. F
15. C
16. J

page 21
1. A
2. Answers will vary. Possible answer: The story is funny. It describes something that could never actually happen.

page 22
1. C
2. Answers will vary. Possible answer: The passage contains facts and explanations.

page 23
1. C
2. G

page 24
1. C
2. J

page 25
1. A
2. J

page 27
1. C
2. F
3. B
4. H
5. A
6. J

page 28
1. C
2. H
3. D
4. H
5. Answers will vary. Possible answer: You can identify each kind of spider by the web it weaves.

page 29
1. D
2. J

page 31
1. D
2. G
3. B
4. G
5. B
6. F

page 32
1. D
2. H

page 33
1. A
2. G
3. B
4. J
5. D
6. F
7. C
8. J

page 34
1. B
2. H
3. D

page 35
1. The main characters are Juan and Bill.
2. The story takes place at Juan's house.
3. The story takes place in the present.
4. Juan has not seen Bill for six months. He's not sure if they will still feel like good friends.
5. Juan keeps checking the clock. He paces the floor and wonders if he and Bill are still friends.

6. Juan tries to act calm and pretend that Bill never moved away.

page 37
1. C
2. G
3. B
4. F
5. C
6. F

page 39
1. C
2. H
3. A
4. H
5. D
6. G
7. B

page 40
1. C
2. F
3. Answers will vary. Possible answer: having a proud family history; being gentle and good

page 41
1. B
2. G
3. D
4. Answers will vary. Possible answer: It would contain facts about the sun and the moon. It wouldn't be told as a story. The sun and moon wouldn't be able to speak or have thoughts.

page 42
1. B
2. F

3. C
4. J

page 43
1. C
2. H
3. B
4. G

page 44
1. C
2. G
3. B
4. G

page 46
1. A
2. G
3. D
4. J
5. B
6. G

page 47
1. C
2. G

page 48
3. A
4. H
5. A
6. F
7. Answers will vary. Possible answer: As more farms are created, it will be harder for cheetahs to hunt and survive.

page 49
1. B
2. G
3. A
4. F

page 51
1. B
2. H
3. A
4. H
5. Answers will vary.

page 52
1. B
2. H
3. A
4. Answers will vary. Possible answer: We could lose sources of medicine if the forests are cleared. Many plants, animals, and insects will lose their natural habitats.

page 54
1. B
2. H
3. A
4. J
5. Answers will vary.

page 55
1. C
2. H
3. D
4. G

page 56
5. B
6. H
7. A
8. H

page 57
1. C
2. F
3. D
4. H
5. A
6. F
7. D

page 58
8. F
9. B
10. H
11. B
12. G

13. D
14. H

page 59
15. B
16. H
17. D
18. H
19. B
20. F
21. C
22. J

page 60
1. B
2. F
3. C

page 61
4. H
5. B
6. H
7. D

page 63
8. H
9. D
10. G
11. C
12. H
13. C

page 65
14. J
15. C
16. F
17. B
18. F
19. D

page 66
20. J
21. C
22. G
23. B

page 67
1. A
2. H
3. C
4. J
5. C
6. F

page 68
1. D
2. G
3. A
4. H
5. B
6. J
7. A

page 69
1. C
2. F
3. B
4. H
5. C

page 70
1. C
2. H
3. C
4. H
5. A

page 71
1. B
2. J
3. B
4. H
5. A
6. G

page 72
1. A
2. G
3. B
4. G
5. D
6. H
7. D
8. G
9. A
10. G
11. D
12. G

page 73
1. D
2. G
3. B
4. H
5. C
6. F

7. D
8. H
9. C

page 74
1. C
2. H
3. D
4. G
5. B
6. H
7. D

page 75
8. G
9. B
10. H
11. D
12. H
13. A
14. H
15. A
16. G
17. D
18. F
19. D

page 76
1. D
2. H
3. B
4. H
5. B
6. J

page 77
1. B
2. J
3. C
4. G
5. A
6. F

page 78
1. B
2. J
3. C
4. J
5. A
6. J

page 79
1. B

2. H
3. B
4. F
5. B
6. H

page 80
1. D
2. F
3. C
4. G
5. B
6. H

page 81
1. A
2. G
3. D
4. H
5. C
6. J

page 82
1. B
2. H
3. D
4. F
5. D
6. J

page 83
7. B
8. F
9. B
10. H
11. D
12. F
13. A

page 84
1. A
2. G
3. B
4. J
5. C
6. G
7. C

page 85
1. A
2. H
3. C
4. H

5. B
6. J
7. C

page 86
1. A
2. H
3. D
4. F
5. A

page 87
1. D
2. J
3. C
4. G
5. B
6. H
7. C
8. G

page 88
1. C
2. F
3. C
4. F
5. B

page 89
1. C
2. G
3. A
4. J

page 90
1. C
2. G

page 91
1. A
2. F
3. A
4. G

page 92
1. A
2. H
3. D
4. H

page 93
1. C
2. F
3. C

4. J
5. D
6. G

page 94
1. D
2. H
3. C
4. J
5. C
6. G

page 95
1. A
2. H
3. D
4. F
5. B

page 96
1. B
2. C
3. A
4. D
5. C
6. D
7. B
8. A
9. D
10. C
11. B
12. B
13. J

page 97
1. A
2. J
3. B
4. G
5. C

page 98
6. G
7. C
8. F
9. D
10. G
11. C
12. J

page 99
13. D
14. F

15. C

page 100
16. J
17. A
18. H
19. B

page 101
20. H
21. A
22. H
23. A
24. G
25. C
26. F
27. D

page 102
28. J
29. C
30. J
31. A
32. J
33. A

page 103
1. Ms. Warner; she asked Jason what was wrong and made a phone call
2. Jason; he forgot his lunch
3. Jason' mother; she brought Jason's lunch to school
4. All three passages describe the morning that Jason forgot to bring his lunch to school.

page 104
1. Answers will vary.
2. Answers will vary.
3. Answers will

vary. Students should identify their audience and follow a specific form of writing.

page 105
Students' paragraphs should have a main idea, supporting details, and a conclusion.

page 106
1. A
2. J
3. warm; winter
   Details: Ants dig into the ground. Female grasshoppers lay their eggs and die. Bees gather in their hive.

page 107
Answers will vary. The paragraph should include transitional words between the steps of the process.

page 108
Answers will vary. Students should write the same procedure using numbered steps.

page 109
Answers will vary. Students should support their choices with reasons.

page 110
1. Answers will vary. The paragraph should include a main idea, details, and a conclusion.

2. Answers will vary. The explanation should include transitional words.

page 111
1. B
2. F
3. C
4. J
5. B
6. F
7. B
8. J

page 112
9. A
10. H
11. D
12. H
13. D
14. G
15. A
16. G
17. D

page 113
18. G
19. A
20. J
21. C
22. H

page 114
23. A
24. J
25. C
26. F
27. B
28. G
29. D
30. F
31. C

page 115
32. J
33. C
34. F
35. A
36. J

37. D
38. H
39. C
40. F
41. A
42. G
43. D
44. G

page 116
1. A
2. H
3. B
4. J
5. B
6. F
7. A

page 117
8. H
9. A
10. H
11. B
12. F
13. B
14. G
15. B
16. J

page 118
1. D
2. H
3. A
4. H
5. A

page 119
6. F
7. C
8. J
9. A

page 120
10. J
11. D
12. J
13. D
14. H
15. B
16. G
17. B
18. F

page 121
19. B
20. F
21. C
22. G
23. J
24. F

page 122
1. Answers will vary. The paragraph should be written in the first-person point of view.
2. Answers will vary. The paragraph should be written in the third-person point of view.

page 123
1. C
2. G
3. C
4. F
5. A

page 124
1. C
2. H
3. D
4. G
5. B
6. G
7. B
8. J

page 125
1. C
2. G
3. C
4. G
5. B
6. H

page 126
1. B
2. H
3. A

4. J
5. A
6. G

page 127
1. D
2. H
3. C
4. F
5. C
6. G

page 128
1. B
2. H
3. B
4. F
5. D
6. F
7. C

page 129
1. D
2. G
3. B
4. G
5. B
6. H

page 130
1. D
2. H
3. A
4. J
5. A
6. G

page 131
1. C
2. J
3. B
4. H
5. C
6. F
7. C
8. G

page 132
1. B
2. H
3. D
4. H
5. A

page 133
1. A
2. G
3. C
4. G
5. A
6. J

page 134
1. B
2. H
3. A
4. G
5. D
6. J

page 135
1. C
2. J
3. B
4. G
5. A
6. J

page 136
1. 12, 27, 13, 45; subtract 10
2. 90, 46, 25, 42; add 9
3. 15, 17, 50, 30; divide by 2

page 137
1. 24, 33, 17; add 5
2. 38, 22, 37; add 8
3. 52, 26, 55; subtract 2
4. 32, 50, 90; subtract 20

page 138
1. D
2. H
3. B
4. J

page 139
1. C
2. F
3. C
4. H

5. A
6. J

page 140
1. D
2. J
3. B
4. G
5. B
6. H
7. C

page 141
1. A
2. J
3. D
4. H
5. D
6. G

page 142
1. B
2. J
3. C
4. G
5. D
6. F

page 143
1. D
2. H
3. B
4. F
5. C
6. J
7. D
8. H

page 144
1. D
2. J
3. B
4. H
5. C

page 145
1. B
2. J
3. C
4. G
5. D
6. G

page 146
1. A
2. F
3. D
4. G
5. B
6. G
7. D
8. F

page 147
1. C
2. G
3. A
4. J
5. B
6. J

page 148
7. D
8. G
9. C
10. H
11. D
12. H
13. A

page 149
14. H
15. D
16. H
17. B
18. J
19. A
20. F

page 150
21. B
22. G
23. B
24. J
25. C
26. G
27. D

page 151
1. C
2. G
3. C
4. J
5. A
6. G

7. D
8. H

page 152
1. C
2. J
3. B
4. H
5. D
6. F
7. A
8. G
9. C
10. J

page 153
1. C
2. H
3. A
4. J
5. B
6. G
7. A
8. F

page 154
1. D
2. H
3. B
4. F
5. A
6. G
7. D
8. H

page 155
1. B
2. J
3. D
4. G
5. A
6. G
7. C
8. H

page 156
1. C
2. J
3. B
4. J
5. A
6. H

7. B
8. H

page 157
1. A
2. J
3. C
4. H
5. C
6. G
7. D
8. F
9. C
10. H

page 158
1. C
2. F
3. D
4. F
5. B
6. F
7. A

page 159
1. B
2. H
3. C
4. H
5. A
6. G
7. A
8. H

page 160
1. D
2. H
3. A
4. H
5. B
6. H
7. D
8. G

page 161
1. A
2. G
3. C
4. J
5. D
6. G
7. A

8. H

page 162
1. C
2. F
3. B
4. H
5. A
6. F
7. D
8. J
9. B
10. H

page 163
1. D
2. H
3. B
4. G
5. D
6. G
7. A
8. F
9. B
10. G

page 164
1. B
2. F
3. B
4. G
5. C
6. J
7. C
8. H
9. B
10. H

page 165
1. C
2. F
3. D
4. J
5. B
6. J
7. D

page 166
1. C
2. F
3. C
4. G

5. D
6. F
7. D
8. H

page 167
1. A
2. G
3. C
4. H
5. A
6. J

page 168
1. B
2. F
3. C
4. F
5. C
6. G
7. A
8. G

page 169
1. C
2. G
3. A
4. G
5. D
6. F

page 170
1. D
2. G
3. C
4. H
5. B

page 171
1. A
2. F
3. B
4. G
5. D
6. F
7. D

page 172
1. B
2. H
3. D
4. F

5. D
6. J

page 173
1. C
2. F
3. A
4. H
5. C
6. J
7. D
8. F
9. B

page 174
10. F
11. B
12. H
13. C
14. H
15. B
16. F
17. C
18. G
19. B
20. G
21. C

page 175
22. J
23. C
24. F
25. C
26. H
27. A
28. G
29. B
30. G
31. B
32. H
33. D

page 176
34. G
35. D
36. F
37. B
38. H
39. C
40. G
41. A

page 177
1. C
2. J
3. A
4. J
5. D

page 178
1. rotation
2. reflection
3. reflection
4. rotation
5. rotation
6. reflection

page 179
1. B
2. G
3. C
4. H

page 180
1. D
2. G
3. C
4. H
5. D

page 181
1. B
2. H
3. B
4. J
5. A
6. H

page 182
1. B
2. J
3. A
4. G
5. D
6. F

page 183
1. C
2. F
3. D
4. J
5. C

page 184
1. line drawn to the

rectangle
2. line drawn to the octagon and rectangle
3. line drawn to the triangle
4. line drawn to the square
5. line drawn to the circle
6. line drawn to the pentagon and rectangle
7. Answers will vary. Students should list items in their house or classroom and identify the appropriate 2-D shape.

page 185
1. Answers will vary but should reflect the instructions.
2. Answers will vary but should reflect the instructions.
3. Answers will vary but should reflect the instructions.
4. Answers will vary but should reflect the instructions.
5. Answers will vary but should reflect the instructions.

page 186
1. D
2. F
3. C
4. F

page 187
1. D
2. F
3. A
4. H
5. D
6. H

page 188

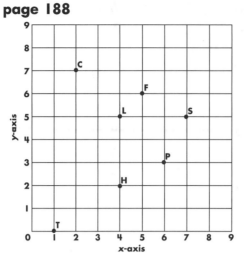

page 189
Point *S* (7, 7),
Point *K* (4, 5),
Point *P* (6,3),
Point *B* (8,2),
Point *J* (1,8),
Point *M* (3,8),
Point *C* (3,3)

page 190
1. D
2. J
3. A
4. H

page 191
5. B
6. F
7. C
8. F
9. D
10. G

page 192
1. C
2. J
3. B
4. G

page 193
1. A
2. F
3. B
4. J
5. C

page 194
1. A
2. J
3. C
4. H
5. B
6. G

page 195
1. 21
2. 2
3. 2
4. 52,800
5. 5
6. 10
7. 62
8. 36

page 196
1. C
2. G
3. C
4. F
5. D
6. J

page 197
1. 340 mm
2. yes
3. 300 cm
4. no
5. 1,000 cm × 1,200 cm

page 198
1. 300
2. 5
3. 230

4. 1; 68
5. 33,000
6. 88
7. 1,000
8. 12,062
9. 5; 2

page 199
1. C
2. G
3. A
4. H
5. B
6. H

page 200
1. C
2. J
3. B
4. F
5. D

page 201
1. D
2. J
3. D
4. F
5. B

page 202
1. D
2. G
3. D
4. H
5. A

page 203
1. A
2. G
3. C
4. J
5. D

page 204
1. D
2. J
3. B
4. F
5. D

page 205
1. A
2. G
3. A
4. F
5. B

page 206
1. B
2. H
3. A
4. H
5. D
6. H

page 207
7. C
8. H
9. C
10. G
11. D
12 H

page 208
1. A
2. J
3. C
4. J

page 209
1. A
2. G
3. C
4. H
5. B

page 210
1. C
2. G
3. A
4. H
5. D
6. H

page 211
1. C
2. F
3. D
4. G
5. C

page 212
1. B
2. G
3. A
4. G
5. C
6. H

page 213
1. C
2. J
3. B
4. G

page 214
1. B
2. F
3. B
4. J
5. C

page 215
1. A
2. H
3. D
4. H
5. A
6. H

page 216
1. D
2. G
3. B
4. H
5. D
6. H

page 217
1. C
2. H
3. D
4. F
5. B
6. G

page 218
1. D
2. G
3. D
4. J
5. A

page 219
1. B
2. G
3. A
4. F
5. D
6. F

page 220
1. A
2. F
3. B
4. J
5. B

page 221
1. D
2. H
3. A
4. H
5. B
6. J

page 222
1. D
2. H
3. B
4. F
5. B

page 223
1. C
2. G
3. A
4. G
5. D

page 224
1. D
2. H
3. 5, 13, 8, 6, 2

page 225
4. bar for size 6 is at 13; bar for size 7 is at 8; bar for size 8 is at 6
5. B
6. G
7. B

page 226
1. C
2. F
3. C
4. G
5. A
6. F

page 227
1. C
2. G
3. A
4. G
5. B
6. F

page 228
1. C
2. G
3. D
4. F
5. B

page 229
1. D
2. F
3. D
4. J
5. C

page 230
1. D
2. F
3. C
4. H
5. A
6. H

page 231
7. A
8. G
9. C
10. H
11. B
12. H

page 232
13. B
14. G
15. C
16. J
17. B
18. H

page 233
19. D
20. H
21. B
22. F
23. C
24. F

page 234
1. C
2. H
3. A
4. H
5. D
6. F
7. A
8. G

page 235
9. A
10. H
11. C
12. F
13. A
14. G
15. B
16. F

page 236
17. A
18. G
19. B
20. F
21. A
22. H
23. B

page 237
24. F
25. B
26. H
27. C
28. 25, 88, 45; divide by 2
29. 62, 40, 56; subtract 3

page 238
30. H
31. A
32. G
33. A

34. F
35. C

page 239
1. A
2. H
3. B
4. G
5. B
6. G
7. A
8. G
9. C
10. J

page 240
11. A
12. J
13. B
14. G
15. C
16. H
17. D
18. H
19. A
20. H

page 241
21. B
22. H
23. D
24. F
25. B
26. G
27. A
28. H

page 242
1. C
2. F
3. A
4. G
5. A

page 243
6. J
7. C
8. G
9. B
10. H
11. B

page 244

12. G
13. B
14. G
15. C
16. J

page 245
17. B
18. J
19. C
20. H
21. C
22. F

page 246
23. B
24. J
25. C
26. J
27. A
28. F